Ninja Foodi Smart XL Grill Cookbook for Beginners 2021

1000-Days Easy & Delicious Indoor Grilling and Air Frying Recipes for Beginners and Advanced Users

Katherine Gust

Table of Contents

Introduction

Ninja Foodi Smart XL Grill is nothing but convenient for those who love to enjoy nicely grilled food but are too busy to set up an outdoor grill every now and then. It has brought innovation right to our fingertips by bringing all the necessary cooking options in a one-touch digital device. It is simple to manage and control. What makes the Ninja Foodi Smart XL Grill stand apart from other grills is the diversity of options it offers for cooking different food items in a single pot. The ceramic coated interior and accessories make grilling an effortless experience. This cookbook puts the idea of the electric grill into perspective by discussing the basics of using the Ninja Foodi Grill. The company has launched the appliance with only one aim that is to provide convenient grilling for all. Try the flavorsome grilling recipes in your Ninja Food grill and experience good taste with amazing aromas, all with little effort and in lesser time. The function of the rheostat and thermostat is to keep the internal temperature of the grill. As with charcoal grills, we are required to maintain it manually with a constant check, whereas in electric grills, the thermostat does that for us. In case of a rise in temperature beyond the set limit, it automatically switches off its circuit to reduce the temperature.

In an electric grill, you are not required to light any fire on your own; it is much less dangerous than other grills. The wiring is completely insulated, and the entire unit is protected with a solid layering on the outside. With a careful understanding of the device, the electric grills prove to be user-friendly and safe to use. Many people believe that electric grills might add a lot to their electricity bills. Though these grills are reliant on electricity, yet they are energy efficient in this regard. About 1760 watts per hour of electricity is used while using an electric grill like Ninja Foodi Grill.

Ninja Foodi Smart XL Grill

The advanced multi-purpose 6 in 1 kitchen miracle Ninja Foodi Smart XL Grill has made grilling an effortless experience. Who knew indoor grilling would become so easy to go someday? But now Ninja Foodi has introduced its mule purpose grill appliance, which allows you to grill, bake, roast, the air crisp, and dehydrate different food items. The device is available in different sizes and models. And each package comes with different accessories and a money-back guarantee.

When you unbox the appliance, you will find plenty of accessories along with the base unit. The base unit is an insulated vessel that has a flip lid attached to one side of the base. When you open the Foodi's lid, there is a hollow space inside for the cooking of the food. For that space, firstly, there is a cooking basket, an air fryer basket, a grill, a grate, and a crisper. Based on the functions of the cooking, these inner baskets are used, which will be discussed in the next section.

Outside the base unit, there is a digital control panel with an LED screen at the center. The screen displays the cooking temperature and internal temperature of the food, plus when to add the food and when the device is preheated. Then there are buttons to select the preset temperature settings and to increase or decrease the cooking timings

The settings for cooking temperature are given according to the MANUAL and PRESET settings. Each mode states a different temperature on the screen. You can either select the temperature and time using the manual settings or select the PRESET to choose from BEEF, POULTRY, and FISH options to automatically select the time and temperature.

Quick User Guide

If you are new to the multipurpose Ninja Foodi Smart XL, then this quick user guide will help you get started with it right away:

For each session of indoor grilling and cooking, you will need to assemble the device accordingly. First, clean both interior and exterior of the grill with a clean cloth. Now plug in the device and press the power button to switch on the device. Open the hood of the Ninja Foodi Grill.

Place the ceramic coated cooking pot inside the grill. This basket is removable and dishwasher safe. Now depending on the cooking mode: Select grill for grilling, air fryer basket for an air fryer, crisper plate for dehydrating, and grate for baking roasting, etc., and place them in the ceramic coated cooking pot of the grill.

The preparation steps include two basic things. Firstly, grease the container of the cooking pot, whether it's the grill, grate, air fryer basket, with a cooking spray to prevent food from sticking. It is a mandatory step, whether the recipe says it or not. Once the internal basket and its accessories are greased with cooking spray, it is time to preheat the device.

Select the mode for cooking by pressing their respective button:

1. Grilling
2. Air Frying
3. Baking
4. Roasting
5. Dehydrating

To start the cooking, cover the lid of the grill, and it will start cooking. As we constantly need to flip the food during grilling, so we can easily open the lid, and it will automatically pause the cooking. The cooking will be resume once we close the lid again. Use the start and stop button to manually initiate and pause cooking. Check when the food's internal temperature reaches the desired level.

Breakfast Recipes

Grilled Bruschetta

Prep Time: 15 minutes.

Cook Time: 4 minutes.

Serves: 4

Ingredients:

- 1 cup celery, chopped
- 1-lb. tomatoes, seeded and chopped
- 3 tablespoons balsamic vinegar
- 1/4 cup basil, minced
- 3 tablespoons olive oil
- 1/2 teaspoon salt
- 2 garlic cloves, minced
- 3 tablespoons Dijon mustard

Mustard Spread

- 1 tablespoon green onion, chopped
- 1/4 cup Dijon mustard
- 1 garlic clove, minced
- 3/4 teaspoon dried oregano
- 1/2 cup mayonnaise
- 1 French loaf bread, sliced

Preparation:

1. Take the first eight ingredients in a bowl and mix them together.
2. Cover this prepared topping and refrigerate for about 30 minutes.
3. Now take mayonnaise, onion, garlic, oregano, and mustard in a bowl.
4. Mix them well and prepare the mayonnaise spread.
5. Place the bread slices in the Ninja Foodi Smart XL grill in batches.
6. Cover the Ninja Foodi Grill's hood, select the Manual Mode, set the temperature to 350 degrees F and grill on the "Grill Mode" for 2 minutes.
7. Flip the bread slices and grill again for 2 minutes.
8. Top the grilled bread with mayonnaise spread and tomato relish.
9. Serve fresh.

Serving Suggestion: Serve the Bruschetta with crispy bacon on the side.

Variation Tip: Add a layer of garlic mayonnaise to the bruschetta.

Nutritional Information Per Serving:

Calories 284 | Fat 7.9g |Sodium 704mg | Carbs 46g | Fiber 3.6g | Sugar 6g | Protein 18g

Grilled Chicken Tacos

Prep Time: 15 minutes.

Cook Time: 18 minutes.

Serves: 4

Ingredients:

- 2 teaspoons sugar
- 1/3 cup olive oil
- 1/3 cup lime juice
- 1/3 cup red wine vinegar
- 2 teaspoons salt
- 2 teaspoons pepper
- 1 cup fresh cilantro, chopped
- 2 tablespoons chipotle in adobo sauce, chopped
- 2 lbs. boneless skinless chicken thighs
- Taco Wraps:
- 8 flour tortillas
- 4 poblano peppers

- 1 tablespoon olive oil
- 2 cups shredded Jack cheese

Preparation:

1. Take the first six ingredients in a blender jug and blend them together.
2. Once blended, mix with chipotles and cilantro.
3. Mix chicken with this cilantro marinade and cover to refrigerate for 8 hours.
4. Grease the poblanos with cooking oil and keep them aside.
5. Place the peppers in the Ninja Foodi Smart XL grill.
6. Cover the Ninja Foodi Grill's hood, select the Manual Mode, set the temperature to 350 degrees F and let them grill on the "Grill Mode" for 2 minutes.
7. Flip the peppers and then continue grilling for another 2 minutes.
8. Place the chicken in the Ninja Foodi Smart XL grill and cover the lid.
9. Grill the chicken for 5 minutes per side, then transfers to a plate.
10. Now peel and slice the peppers in half, then also slice the chicken.
11. Spread each tortilla and add half cup chicken, half peppers, and ¼ cup cheese.
12. Fold the tortilla and carefully place it in the Ninja Foodi Smart XL grill and cover its lid.
13. Grill each for 2 minutes per side on the medium temperature setting.
14. Serve.

Serving Suggestion: Serve the tacos with crumbled crispy bacon on top and warm bread on the side

Variation Tip: Add chopped carrots and cabbage to the chicken filling.

Nutritional Information Per Serving:

Calories 134 | Fat 4.7g |Sodium 1mg | Carbs 54.1g | Fiber 7g | Sugar 3.3g | Protein 26g

Grilled French Toast

Prep Time: 15 minutes.

Cook Time: 8minutes.

Serves: 6

Ingredients:

- 3 eggs
- 1-quart strawberries, quartered
- 2 tablespoons aged balsamic vinegar
- Juice of 1 orange and 2 teaspoons orange zest
- 1 sprig of fresh rosemary
- 3/4 cup heavy cream
- 2 tablespoons honey
- 1 teaspoon vanilla extract
- Salt to taste
- 6- 1-inch challah bread slices
- Fine sugar, for dusting

Preparation:

1. Spread a foil sheet on a working surface.
2. Add strawberries, balsamic, orange juice, rosemary, and zest.
3. Fold the foil edges to make a pocket.
4. Whisk egg with cream, honey, vanilla, and a pinch of salt.
5. Dip and soak the bread slices in this mixture and shake off the excess.
6. Place the bread slices and the foil packet in the Ninja Foodi Smart XL grill.
7. Cover the Ninja Foodi Grill's hood, select the Manual Mode, set the temperature to 350 degrees F and let them grill on the "Grill Mode" for 2 minutes in batches.
8. Flip the bread slices and continue grilling for another 2 minutes.
9. Serve the bread with the strawberry mix on top.
10. Enjoy.

Serving Suggestion: Serve the French toasts with maple syrup.

Variation Tip: Replace honey with maple syrup.

Nutritional Information Per Serving:

Calories 387 | Fat 6g |Sodium 154mg | Carbs 37.4g | Fiber 2.9g | Sugar 15g | Protein 15g

Sausage with Eggs

Prep Time: 15 minutes.

Cook Time: 10 minutes.

Serves: 4

Ingredients:

- 4 sausage links
- 2 cups kale, chopped
- 1 sweet yellow onion, chopped
- 4 eggs
- 1 cup mushrooms
- Olive oil

Preparation:

1. Place the sausages in the Ninja Foodi Smart XL grill.
2. Cover the Ninja Foodi Grill's hood, select the Manual Mode, set the temperature to 375 degrees F and grill on the "Grill Mode" for 2 minutes.
3. Flip the sausages and continue grilling for another 3 minutes
4. Now spread the onion, mushrooms, sausages, and kale in an iron skillet.
5. Crack the eggs in between the sausages.
6. Bake this mixture for 5 minutes in the oven at 350 degrees F.
7. Serve warm and fresh.

Serving Suggestion: Serve the sausages with crispy bread toasts.

Variation Tip: Add chopped tomatoes to the mixture before baking.

Nutritional Information Per Serving:

Calories 212 | Fat 12g |Sodium 321mg | Carbs 14.6g | Fiber 4g | Sugar 8g | Protein 17g

Coffee Glazed Bagels

Prep Time: 15 minutes.

Cook Time: 4 minutes.

Serves: 4

Ingredients:

- 4 bagels split in half
- 1/4 cup coconut milk
- 1 cup fine sugar
- 2 tablespoons black coffee
- 2 tablespoons coconut flakes

Preparation:

1. Place 2 bagels in the Ninja Foodi Smart XL grill.
2. Cover the Ninja Foodi Grill's hood, select the Manual Mode, set the temperature to 325 degrees F and grill on the "Grill Mode" for 2 minutes.
3. Flip the bagel and continue grilling for another 2 minutes.
4. Grill the remaining bagels in a similar way.
5. Whisk the rest of the ingredients in a bowl well.
6. Drizzle this sauce over the grilled bagels.
7. Serve.

Serving Suggestion: Serve the bagels with chocolate syrup.

Variation Tip: Cut the bagels in half and layer them with cream cheese.

Nutritional Information Per Serving:

Calories 412 | Fat 25g |Sodium 132mg | Carbs 44g | Fiber 3.9g | Sugar 3g | Protein 18.9g

Portobello Mushrooms Bruschetta

Prep Time: 15 minutes.

Cook Time: 8 minutes.

Serves: 6

Ingredients:

- 2 cups cherry tomatoes, cut in half
- 3 tablespoons red onion, diced
- 3 tablespoons fresh basil, shredded
- Salt and black pepper to taste
- 4 tablespoons butter
- 1 teaspoon dried oregano
- 6 Portobello Mushrooms caps

Balsamic Glaze

- 2 teaspoons brown sugar
- 1/4 cup balsamic vinegar

Preparation:

1. Start by preparing the balsamic glaze and take all its ingredients in a saucepan.
2. Stir, cook this mixture for 8 minutes on medium heat, then remove from the heat.
3. Take the mushrooms and brush them with the prepared glaze.
4. Stuff the remaining ingredients into the mushrooms.
5. Place the stuffed mushrooms in the Ninja Foodi Smart XL grill with their cap side down.
6. Cover the Ninja Foodi Grill's hood, select the Manual Mode, set the temperature to 350 degrees F and grill on the "Grill Mode" for 8 minutes.
7. Serve.

Serving Suggestion: Serve the mushrooms with fried eggs and crispy bacon.

Variation Tip: Add chopped parsley to the mushrooms

Nutritional Information Per Serving:

Calories 331 | Fat 2.5g |Sodium 595mg | Carbs 19g | Fiber 12g | Sugar 12g | Protein 8.7g

Avocado Eggs

Prep Time: 15 minutes.

Cook Time: 5 minutes.

Serves: 2

Ingredients:

- 2 eggs
- 1 ripe avocado
- 1 pinch of barbecue rub
- Salt and pepper, to taste

Preparation:

1. Slice the avocado in half and remove its pit.
2. Remove some flesh from the center.
3. Drizzle barbecue rub, salt, and black pepper on top.
4. Place the avocado in the Ninja Foodi Smart XL grill with their skin side down.
5. Cover the Ninja Foodi Grill's hood, select the Manual Mode, set the temperature to 350 degrees F and grill on the "Grill Mode" for 8 minutes.
6. Flip the avocados once grilled half-way through.
7. Crack an egg into each half of the avocado.
8. Serve.

Serving Suggestion: Serve the avocado cups with crispy bacon on top.

Variation Tip: Top egg with chopped bell pepper and fresh herbs.

Nutritional Information Per Serving:

Calories 322 | Fat 12g |Sodium 202mg | Carbs 14.6g | Fiber 4g | Sugar 8g | Protein 17.3g

Bacon-Herb Grit

Prep Time: 15 minutes.

Cook Time: 10 minutes.

Serves: 4

Ingredients:

- 2 teaspoons fresh parsley, chopped
- 1/2 teaspoon garlic powder
- 1/2 teaspoon black pepper
- 3 bacon slices, cooked and crumbled
- 1/2 cup cheddar cheese, shredded
- 4 cups instant grits
- Cooking spray

Preparation:

1. Start by mixing the first seven ingredients in a suitable bowl.
2. Spread this mixture in a 10-inch baking pan and refrigerate for 1 hour.
3. Flip the pan on a plate and cut the grits mixture into 4 triangles.
4. Place the grit slices in the Ninja Foodi Smart XL grill.
5. Cover the Ninja Foodi Grill's hood, select the Manual Mode, set the temperature to 350 degrees F and grill on the "Grill Mode" for 5 minutes per side.
6. serve

Serving Suggestion: Serve these grits with hot sauce or any other tangy sauce you like.

Variation Tip: Add sautéed ground chicken or pork.

Nutritional Information Per Serving:

Calories 197 | Fat 15g |Sodium 548mg | Carbs 59g | Fiber 4g | Sugar 1g | Protein 7.9g

Snacks and Appetizer Recipes

Cob with Pepper Butter

Prep Time: 15 minutes.

Cook Time: 15 minutes.

Serves: 8

Ingredients:

- 8 medium ears sweet corn
- 1 cup butter, softened
- 2 tablespoons lemon-pepper seasoning

Preparation:

1. Season the corn cob with butter and lemon pepper liberally.
2. Place the corn cob in the Ninja Foodi Smart XL grill.
3. Cover the Ninja Foodi Grill's hood, select the Manual Mode, set the temperature to 360 degrees F and grill on the "Grill Mode" for 15 minutes while rotating after every 5 minutes.
4. Grill the corn cobs in batches.
5. Serve warm.

Serving Suggestion: Serve the corn with parsley on top.

Variation Tip: Coat the corn with crushed cornflakes after grilling.

Nutritional Information Per Serving:

Calories 218 | Fat 22g | Sodium 350mg | Carbs 32.2g | Fiber 0.7g | Sugar 1g | Protein 4.3g

Grilled Eggplant

Prep Time: 15 minutes.

Cook Time: 10 minutes.

Serves: 4

Ingredients:

- 2 small eggplants, half-inch slices
- 1/4 cup olive oil
- 2 tablespoons lime juice
- 3 teaspoons Cajun seasoning

Preparation:

1. Liberally season the eggplant slices with oil, lemon juice, and Cajun seasoning.
2. Place the eggplant slices in the Ninja Foodi Smart XL grill.
3. Cover the Ninja Foodi Grill's hood, select the Manual Mode, set the temperature to 375 degrees F and grill on the "Grill Mode" for 5 minutes per side.
4. Serve.

Serving Suggestion: Serve the grilled eggplant with cucumber dip.

Variation Tip: Drizzle breadcrumbs on top and press before grilling.

Nutritional Information Per Serving:

Calories 157 | Fat 2g |Sodium 48mg | Carbs 16g | Fiber 2g | Sugar 0g | Protein 7g

Tarragon Asparagus

Prep Time: 15 minutes.

Cook Time: 16 minutes.

Serves: 4

Ingredients:

- 2 lbs. fresh asparagus, trimmed
- 2 tablespoons olive oil
- 1 teaspoon salt
- 1/2 teaspoon black pepper
- 1/4 cup honey
- 4 tablespoons fresh tarragon, minced

Preparation:

1. Liberally season the asparagus by tossing it with oil, salt, pepper, honey, and tarragon.

2. Place the asparagus in the Ninja Foodi Smart XL grill.

3. Cover the Ninja Foodi Grill's hood, select the Manual Mode, set the temperature to 325 degrees F and grill on the "Grill Mode" for 8 minutes per side, give them a toss after 4 minutes.

4. Serve warm.

Serving Suggestion: Serve the asparagus with crispy bacon.

Variation Tip: Coat the asparagus with breadcrumbs before cooking.

Nutritional Information Per Serving:

Calories 104 | Fat 3g |Sodium 216mg | Carbs 17g | Fiber 3g | Sugar 4g | Protein 1g

Grilled Butternut Squash

Prep Time: 15 minutes.

Cook Time: 16 minutes.

Serves: 4

Ingredients:

- 1 medium butternut squash
- 1 tablespoon olive oil
- 1 ½ teaspoons dried oregano
- 1 teaspoon dried thyme
- 1/2 teaspoon salt
- 1/4 teaspoon black pepper

Preparation:

1. Peel and slice the squash into ½ inch thick slices.
2. Remove the center of the slices to discard the seeds.
3. Toss the squash slices with the remaining ingredients in a bowl.
4. Place the squash in the Ninja Foodi Smart XL grill.
5. Cover the Ninja Foodi Grill's hood, select the Manual Mode, set the temperature to 325 degrees F and grill on the "Grill Mode" for 8 minutes per side.
6. Serve warm.

Serving Suggestion: Serve the squash with chili sauce or mayonnaise dip.

Variation Tip: Added shredded cheese on top of the grilled squash.

Nutritional Information Per Serving:

Calories 180 | Fat 9g |Sodium 318mg | Carbs 19g | Fiber 5g | Sugar 3g | Protein 7g

Honey Glazed Bratwurst

Prep Time: 15 minutes.

Cook Time: 20 minutes.

Serves: 4

Ingredients:

- 4 bratwurst links, uncooked
- 1/4 cup Dijon mustard
- 1/4 cup honey
- 2 tablespoons mayonnaise
- 1 teaspoon steak sauce
- 4 brat buns, split

Preparation:

1. First, mix the mustard with steak sauce and mayonnaise in a bowl.
2. Place the bratwurst in the Ninja Foodi Smart XL grill.
3. Cover the Ninja Foodi Grill's hood, select the Manual Mode, set the temperature to 350 degrees F and grill on the "Grill Mode" for 10 minutes per side until their internal temperature reaches 165 degrees F.
4. Serve with buns and mustard sauce on top.

Serving Suggestion: Serve the bratwurst with crumbled nacho chips on top and a cream cheese dip on the side.

Variation Tip: Toss bratwurst with shredded parmesan before serving.

Nutritional Information Per Serving:

Calories 173 | Fat 8g |Sodium 146mg | Carbs 18g | Fiber 5g | Sugar 1g | Protein 7g

Chicken Salad with Blueberry Vinaigrette

Prep Time: 15 minutes.

Cook Time: 14 minutes.

Serves: 4

Ingredients:

Salads:

- 1 package (10 oz.) salad greens
- 1 cup fresh blueberries
- 1/2 cup canned oranges
- 1 cup goat cheese, crumbled

Chicken:

- 2 boneless chicken breasts, halves
- 1 tablespoon olive oil
- 1 garlic clove, minced
- 1/4 teaspoon salt
- 1/4 teaspoon black pepper

Vinaigrette:

- 1/4 cup olive oil
- 1/4 cup blueberry preserves
- 2 tablespoons balsamic vinegar
- 2 tablespoons maple syrup
- 1/4 teaspoon ground mustard
- 1/8 teaspoon salt
- Dash pepper

Preparation:

1. First, season the chicken liberally with garlic, salt, pepper, and oil in a bowl.
2. Cover to refrigerate for 30 minutes margination.
3. Place the chicken in the Ninja Foodi Smart XL grill.
4. Cover the Ninja Foodi Grill's hood, select the Manual Mode, set the temperature to 350 degrees F and grill on the "Grill Mode" for 5-7 minutes per side until the internal temperature reaches 330 degrees F.
5. Toss the remaining ingredients for salad and vinaigrette in a bowl.
6. Slice the grilled chicken and serve with salad.

Serving Suggestion: Serve the chicken salad with fresh berries on top.

Variation Tip: Add shredded cheese and strawberries to the salad.

Nutritional Information Per Serving:

Calories 140 | Fat 5g |Sodium 244mg | Carbs 16g | Fiber 1g | Sugar 1g | Protein 17g

Pineapple with Cream Cheese Dip

Prep Time: 15 minutes.

Cook Time: 8 minutes.

Serves: 4

Ingredients:

Pineapple

- 1 fresh pineapple
- 1/4 cup packed brown sugar
- 3 tablespoons honey
- 2 tablespoons lime juice

Dip

- 3 oz. cream cheese softened
- 1/4 cup yogurt
- 2 tablespoons honey
- 1 tablespoon brown sugar
- 1 tablespoon lime juice
- 1 teaspoon lime zest, grated

Preparation:

1. First, slice the peeled pineapple into 8 wedges, then cut each wedge into 2 spears.
2. Toss the pineapple with sugar, lime juice, and honey in a bowl, then refrigerate for 1 hour.
3. Meanwhile, prepare the lime dip by whisking all its ingredients together in a bowl.
4. Remove the pineapple from its marinade.
5. Place the pineapple in the Ninja Foodi Smart XL grill.
6. Cover the Ninja Foodi Grill's hood, select the Manual Mode, set the temperature to 375 degrees F and grill on the "Grill Mode" for 4 minutes per side.
7. Serve with lime dip.

Serving Suggestion: Serve the pineapple with cream cheese dip.

Variation Tip: Toss the grilled pineapples with berries.

Nutritional Information Per Serving:

Calories 282 | Fat 4g |Sodium 232mg | Carbs 47g | Fiber 1g | Sugar 0g | Protein 4g

Bacon Hot Dogs

Prep Time: 15 minutes.

Cook Time: 6 minutes.

Serves: 8

Ingredients:

- 12 bacon strips
- 8 beef hot dogs
- 8 hot dog buns, split and toasted
- 1/4 cup chopped red onion
- 2 cups sauerkraut, rinsed and drained

Preparation:

1. Sear the bacon in a skillet until crispy from both sides.
2. Wrap a bacon strip around each hot dog and secure it by inserting a toothpick.
3. Place the hot dogs in the Ninja Foodi Smart XL grill.
4. Cover the Ninja Foodi Grill's hood, select the Manual Mode, set the temperature to 375 degrees F and grill on the "Grill Mode" for 6 minutes while rotating after every 2 minutes.
5. Cook all the hot dogs in batches, then remove the toothpick.
6. Serve warm in a hotdog bun with sauerkraut and onion.
7. Enjoy.

Serving Suggestion: Serve the hotdogs with tomato sauce or mayo dip.

Variation Tip: Add mustard sauce to hotdogs.

Nutritional Information Per Serving:

Calories 229 | Fat 5g |Sodium 510mg | Carbs 37g | Fiber 5g | Sugar 4g | Protein 11g

Grilled Oysters with Chorizo Butter

Prep Time: 15 minutes.

Cook Time: 2 minutes.

Serves: 6

Ingredients:

- 4 ounces Mexican chorizo
- 1 ½ sticks butter, cut into cubes
- 2 tablespoons fresh lime juice
- Salt, to taste
- 18 Louisiana oysters, scrubbed
- Cilantro leaves and lime zest for garnish

Preparation:

1. Sauté chorizo with butter and lime juice and salt in a skillet for 8 minutes until brown.
2. Transfer the sautéed chorizo to a plate.
3. Place the oysters in the Ninja Foodi Smart XL grill.
4. Cover the Ninja Foodi Grill's hood, select the Manual Mode, set the temperature to 325 degrees F and grill on the "Grill Mode" for 2 minutes.
5. Divide the chorizo on top of the grilled oysters.
6. Serve warm.

Serving Suggestion: Serve the oysters with garlic butter.

Variation Tip: Drizzle paprika on top for more spice.

Nutritional Information Per Serving:

Calories 201 | Fat 7g |Sodium 269mg | Carbs 15g | Fiber 4g | Sugar 12g | Protein 26g

Cheese-Stuffed Grilled Peppers

Prep Time: 15 minutes.

Cook Time: 7 minutes.

Serves: 4

Ingredients:

- 1 cup ricotta cheese
- 1 cup cream cheese
- 1/2 cup Parmigiano-Reggiano cheese, grated
- Salt and black pepper, to taste
- 4 Anaheim or Cubanelle peppers
- 4 baby bell peppers
- 4 small poblano chiles
- Olive oil, for rubbing

Preparation:

1. Mix cream cheese, ricotta, black pepper, salt, and Parmigiano-Reggiano in a bowl.
2. Remove the top of the peppers and stuff them with ricotta mixture.
3. Place the peppers in the Ninja Foodi Smart XL grill.
4. Cover the Ninja Foodi Grill's hood, select the Manual Mode, set the temperature to 375 degrees F and grill on the "Grill Mode" for 7 minutes.
5. Serve warm.

Serving Suggestion: Serve the peppers with chili garlic sauce.

Variation Tip: Add pepperoni and sliced olives to the filling.

Nutritional Information Per Serving:

Calories 148 | Fat 12g | Sodium 710mg | Carbs 14g | Fiber 5g | Sugar 3g | Protein 11g

Grilled Zucchini with Fresh Mozzarella

Prep Time: 15 minutes.

Cook Time: 10 minutes.

Serves: 6

Ingredients:

- 3 zucchinis, cut into slices
- 2 tablespoons olive oil
- Salt, to taste
- Black pepper, to taste
- 1/4 teaspoon wine vinegar
- 1 garlic clove, minced
- 1 tablespoon parsley, chopped
- ½ pound fresh mozzarella, cut into thick slices

Preparation:

1. Toss zucchini with olive oil, black pepper, salt, wine vinegar, garlic, and parsley in a bowl.
2. Place the zucchini slices in the Ninja Foodi Smart XL grill.
3. Cover the Ninja Foodi Grill's hood, select the Manual Mode, set the temperature to 400 degrees F and grill on the "Grill Mode" for 5 minutes per side.
4. Serve the zucchini slices with the cheese.
5. Enjoy.

Serving Suggestion: Serve the zucchini with yogurt dip.

Variation Tip: Coat the zucchini with breadcrumbs before cooking.

Nutritional Information Per Serving:

Calories 175 | Fat 16g |Sodium 255mg | Carbs 31g | Fiber 1.2g | Sugar 5g | Protein 24.1g

Poultry Mains

Chicken and Tomatoes

Prep Time: 15 minutes.

Cook Time: 10 minutes.

Serves: 4

Ingredients:

- 2 tablespoons olive oil
- 1 garlic clove, minced
- 1/2 teaspoon salt
- 1/4 cup fresh basil leaves
- 8 plum tomatoes
- 3/4 cup vinegar
- 4 chicken breast, boneless skinless

Preparation:

1. Take the first five ingredients together in a blender jug.
2. Blend them well, then add four tomatoes to blend again.
3. Take chicken in a suitable bowl and pour 2/3 cup of the prepared marinade.
4. Mix well and refrigerate the chicken for 1 hour.
5. Place the 2 chicken pieces in the Ninja Foodi Smart XL grill.
6. Cover the Ninja Foodi Grill's hood, select the Manual Mode, set the temperature to 350 degrees F and grill on the "Grill Mode" for 5 minutes.
7. Flip the grilled chicken and continue grilling until it is al dente.
8. Cook the remaining chicken in a similar way.
9. Serve.

Serving Suggestion: Serve the chicken and tomatoes with a kale salad on the side.

Variation Tip: Add lemon juice for a refreshing taste.

Nutritional Information Per Serving:

Calories 335 | Fat 25g |Sodium 122mg | Carbs 13g | Fiber 0.4g | Sugar 1g | Protein 33g

Spinach Turkey Burgers

Prep Time: 15 minutes.

Cook Time: 19 minutes.

Serves: 8

Ingredients:

- 1 tablespoon avocado oil
- 2 lbs. turkey ground
- 2 shallots, chopped
- 2 ½ cups spinach, chopped
- 3 garlic cloves, minced
- 2/3 cup feta cheese, crumbled
- 3/4 teaspoon Greek seasoning
- 1/2 teaspoon salt
- 1/4 teaspoon black pepper
- 8 hamburger buns, split

Preparation:

1. Start by sautéing shallots in a skillet for 2 minutes, then add garlic and spinach.
2. Cook for 45 seconds, then transfers to a suitable bowl.
3. Add all the seasoning, beef, and feta cheese to the bowl.
4. Mix well, then make 8 patties of ½ inch thickness.
5. Place 2 patties in the Ninja Foodi Smart XL grill.
6. Cover the Ninja Foodi Grill's hood, select the Manual Mode, set the temperature to 350 degrees F and grill on the "Grill Mode" for 8 minutes.
7. Flip the patties and continue grilling for another 8 minutes.
8. Grill the remaining patties in a similar way.
9. Serve the patties in between the buns with desired toppings.
10. Enjoy.

Serving Suggestion: Serve the burgers with roasted green beans and mashed potatoes.

Variation Tip: Add chopped kale instead of spinach to make the burgers.

Nutritional Information Per Serving:

Calories 529 | Fat 17g | Sodium 422mg | Carbs 55g | Fiber 0g | Sugar 1g | Protein 41g

Montreal Chicken Sandwiches

Prep Time: 15 minutes.

Cook Time: 12 minutes.

Serves: 4

Ingredients:

- 1/4 cup mayonnaise
- 1 tablespoon Dijon mustard
- 1 tablespoon honey
- 4 chicken breasts, halves
- 1/2 teaspoon Montreal seasoning
- 4 slices Swiss cheese
- 4 hamburger buns, split
- 2 bacon strips, cooked and crumbled
- Lettuce leaves and tomato slices, optional

Preparation:

1. First, lb. the chicken with a mallet into ½ inch thickness.
2. Now season it with steak seasoning and rub it well.
3. Place 2 chicken pieces in the Ninja Foodi Smart XL grill.
4. Cover the Ninja Foodi Grill's hood, select the Manual Mode, set the temperature to 350 degrees F and grill on the "Grill Mode" for 6 minutes.
5. Flip the chicken and continue grilling for another 6 minutes.
6. Cook the remaining chicken in a similar way.
7. Mix mayonnaise with honey and mustard in a bowl
8. Place the one chicken piece on top of each half of the bun.
9. Top it with a mayo mixture, 1 cheese slice, and other toppings.
10. Place the other bun halve on top.
11. Serve.

Serving Suggestion: Serve the sandwiches with roasted veggies.

Variation Tip: Replace chicken with the turkey meat to make these sandwiches

Nutritional Information Per Serving:

Calories 284 | Fat 25g |Sodium 460mg | Carbs 36g | Fiber 0.4g | Sugar 2g | Protein 26g

Sriracha Wings

Prep Time: 15 minutes.

Cook Time: 25 minutes.

Serves: 6

Ingredients:

- 12 chicken wings
- 1 tablespoon canola oil
- 2 teaspoons ground coriander
- 1/2 teaspoon garlic salt
- 1/4 teaspoon black pepper

Glaze

- 1/2 cup orange juice
- 1/3 cup Sriracha chili sauce
- 1/4 cup butter, cubed
- 3 tablespoons honey
- 2 tablespoons lime juice
- 1/4 cup fresh cilantro, chopped

Preparation:

1. Season the wings with all their seasoning in a suitable bowl.
2. Mix well, then cover to refrigerate for 2 hours of marination.
3. Meanwhile, prepare the sauce by cooking its ingredients in a saucepan for 4 minutes.
4. Place the chicken wings in the Ninja Foodi Smart XL grill.
5. Cover the Ninja Foodi Grill's hood, select the Manual Mode, set the temperature to 375 degrees F and grill on the "Grill Mode" for 15 minutes.
6. Flip the grilled wings and continue cooking for another 10 minutes.
7. Drizzle the prepared sauce over the wings in a bowl.
8. Toss well and serve.

Serving Suggestion: Serve the wings with fresh cucumber and couscous salad.

Variation Tip: Toss the wings, the pork rinds, and the bacon serving.

Nutritional Information Per Serving:

Calories 352 | Fat 2.4g |Sodium 216mg | Carbs 16g | Fiber 2.3g | Sugar 1.2g | Protein 27g

Bourbon Drumsticks

Prep Time: 15 minutes.

Cook Time: 40 minutes.

Serves: 6

Ingredients:

- 1 cup ketchup
- 2 tablespoons brown sugar
- 12 chicken drumsticks
- 2 tablespoons bourbon
- 4 teaspoons barbecue seasoning
- 1 tablespoon Worcestershire sauce
- 2/3 cup Dr. Pepper spice
- 2 teaspoons dried minced onion
- 1/8 teaspoon salt
- 1/4 teaspoon celery salt, optional

Preparation:

1. Take the first eight ingredients in a saucepan.
2. Stir cook for 10 minutes on a simmer until the sauce thickens.
3. Place 6 drumsticks in the Ninja Foodi Smart XL grill and brush it with the sauce.
4. Cover the Ninja Foodi Grill's hood, select the Manual Mode, set the temperature to 400 degrees F and grill on the "Grill Mode" for 10 minutes.
5. Flip the grilled chicken and baste it with the remaining sauce.
6. Continue grilling for another 10 minutes until al dente.
7. Cook the remaining drumsticks in a similar way.
8. Garnish with remaining sauce on top.
9. Serve.

Serving Suggestion: Serve the drumsticks with fresh herbs on top and a bowl of steamed rice.

Variation Tip: Use honey or maple syrup for the marinade.

Nutritional Information Per Serving:

Calories 388 | Fat 8g |Sodium 611mg | Carbs 8g | Fiber 0g | Sugar 4g | Protein 13g

Tomato Turkey Burgers

Prep Time: 15 minutes.

Cook Time: 14 minutes.

Serves: 6

Ingredients:

- 1 large red onion, chopped
- 6 ciabatta rolls, sliced in half
- 1 cup (4 oz.) feta cheese
- 2/3 cup sun-dried tomatoes, chopped
- 1/4 teaspoon salt
- 1/4 teaspoon black pepper
- 2 lbs. lean ground turkey

Preparation:

1. Take all the ingredients for burgers in a bowl except the ciabatta rolls.
2. Mix well and make six patties out of this turkey mixture.
3. Place 2 turkey patties in the Ninja Foodi Smart XL grill.
4. Cover the Ninja Foodi Grill's hood, select the Manual Mode, set the temperature to 350 degrees F and grill on the "Grill Mode" for 7 minutes.
5. Flip the patties and continue grilling for another 7 minutes.
6. Grill the remaining patties in a similar way.
7. Serve with ciabatta rolls.

Serving Suggestion: Serve the turkey meatballs with toasted bread slices.

Variation Tip: Add canned corn kernels to the burgers.

Nutritional Information Per Serving:

Calories 301 | Fat 16g |Sodium 412mg | Carbs 32g | Fiber 0.2g | Sugar 1g | Protein 28.2g

Chicken with Grilled Apples

Prep Time: 15 minutes.

Cook Time: 12 minutes.

Serves: 4

Ingredients:

- 4 chicken breasts, halved
- 4 teaspoons chicken seasoning
- 1 large apple, wedged
- 1 tablespoon lemon juice
- 4 slices provolone cheese
- 1/2 cup Alfredo sauce
- 1/4 cup blue cheese, crumbled

Preparation:

1. Take chicken in a bowl and season it with chicken seasoning.

2. Toss apple with lemon juice in another small bowl.

3. Place the chicken in the Ninja Foodi Smart XL grill.

4. Cover the Ninja Foodi Grill's hood, select the Manual Mode, set the temperature to 350 degrees F and grill on the "Grill Mode" for 8 minutes approximately.

5. Flip the grilled chicken and continue cooking for another 8 minutes.

6. Now grill the apple in the same grill for 2 minutes per side.

7. Serve the chicken with apple, blue cheese, and alfredo sauce.

8. Enjoy.

Serving Suggestion: Serve the chicken with apples with white rice or vegetable chow Mein.

Variation Tip: Wrap the chicken with bacon before grilling for more taste.

Nutritional Information Per Serving:

Calories 231 | Fat 20.1g |Sodium 364mg | Carbs 30g | Fiber 1g | Sugar 1.4g | Protein 15g

Barbecued Turkey

Prep Time: 15 minutes.

Cook Time: 30 minutes.

Serves: 6

Ingredients:

- 1 cup Greek yogurt
- 1/2 cup lemon juice
- 1/3 cup canola oil
- 1/2 cup fresh parsley, minced
- 1 (3 lbs.) turkey breast half, bone-in
- 1/2 cup green onions, chopped
- 4 garlic cloves, minced
- 4 tablespoons dill, fresh minced
- 1 teaspoon dried rosemary, crushed
- 1 teaspoon salt
- 1/2 teaspoon black pepper

Preparation:

1. Take the first 10 ingredients in a bowl and mix well.
2. Mix turkey with this marinade in a suitable bowl for seasoning.
3. Cover it to marinate for 8 hours of marination.
4. Place the turkey in the Ninja Foodi Smart XL grill.
5. Cover the Ninja Foodi Grill's hood, select the Manual Mode, set the temperature to 375 degrees F and grill on the "Grill Mode" for 15 minutes.
6. Flip the turkey and continue grilling for another 15 minutes until al dente.
7. Grill until the internal temperature reaches 350 degrees F.
8. Slice and serve.

Serving Suggestion: Serve the turkey with avocado guacamole.

Variation Tip: Add sweet paprika for a tangy taste.

Nutritional Information Per Serving:

Calories 440 | Fat 14g |Sodium 220mg | Carbs 22g | Fiber 0.2g | Sugar 1g | Protein 37g

Grilled Chicken Breasts with Grapefruit Glaze

Prep Time: 15 minutes.

Cook Time: 16 minutes.

Serves: 4

Ingredients:

- 2 garlic cloves, minced
- 1 teaspoon grapefruit zest
- 1/2 cup grapefruit juice
- 1 tablespoon cooking oil
- 2 tablespoons honey
- 1/2 teaspoon salt
- 1/4 teaspoon black pepper
- 4 bone-in chicken breasts

Preparation:

1. Mix garlic, black pepper, salt, honey, oil, grapefruit juice, and zest in a small saucepan.
2. Cook the grapefruit mixture for 5-7 minutes until it thickens.
3. Place the chicken in the Ninja Foodi Smart XL grill.
4. Cover the Ninja Foodi Grill's hood, select the Manual Mode, set the temperature to 350 degrees F and grill on the "Grill Mode" for 8 minutes per side.
5. Pour this glaze over the chicken breasts.
6. Slice and serve warm.

Serving Suggestion: Serve the chicken breasts with warmed pita bread.

Variation Tip: Add maple syrup instead of honey.

Nutritional Information Per Serving:

Calories 380 | Fat 8g |Sodium 339mg | Carbs 33g | Fiber 1g | Sugar 2g | Protein 21g

Chicken Kebabs with Currants

Prep Time: 15 minutes.

Cook Time: 16 minutes.

Serves: 6

Ingredients:

- 2 medium red bell peppers, cubed
- 1 cup dried currants
- 1 (14-ounce) jar sweet pickled red peppers, cubed
- 1/2 cup of the juices from pickles
- 2 tablespoons olive oil
- Kosher salt, to taste
- 3 pounds boneless chicken thighs, cut into 1-inch-wide strips
- 3 pounds boneless chicken breasts, cut into strips

Preparation:

1. Toss chicken with olive oil, peppers, pickle juices, salt, and currants.
2. Cover and refrigerate the chicken for 30 minutes for marination.
3. Thread the marinated chicken on the wooden skewers.
4. Place the chicken skewers in the Ninja Foodi Smart XL grill.
5. Cover the Ninja Foodi Grill's hood, select the Manual Mode, set the temperature to 375 degrees F and let the skewers grill on the "Grill Mode" for 8 minutes per side.
6. Serve warm.

Serving Suggestion: Serve the chicken kebabs with steaming white rice.

Variation Tip: Add 1 tablespoon lemon juice to the seasoning and marinate.

Nutritional Information Per Serving:

Calories 361 | Fat 16g |Sodium 189mg | Carbs 19.3g | Fiber 0.3g | Sugar 18.2g | Protein 33.3g

Grilled Red Curry Chicken

Prep Time: 15 minutes.

Cook Time: 30 minutes.

Serves: 6

Ingredients:

- 1 (3-pounds) chicken wings, tips removed
- 1/4 cup unsweetened coconut milk
- 2 tablespoons red curry paste
- 1 teaspoon dark brown sugar
- Salt and freshly ground pepper, to taste

Preparation:

1. Mix coconut milk with red curry paste, brown sugar, black pepper, salt in a bowl.
2. Toss in chicken wings and mix well.
3. Cover and marinate the wings for 1 hour in the refrigerator.
4. Place the wings in the Ninja Foodi Smart XL grill.
5. Cover the Ninja Foodi Grill's hood, select the Manual Mode, set the temperature to 350 degrees F and let them grill on the "Grill Mode" for 10 minutes.
6. Flip the wings and grill for 20 minutes.
7. Serve warm.

Serving Suggestion: Serve the curry chicken with a warmed tortilla.

Variation Tip: Add dried herbs to the seasoning.

Nutritional Information Per Serving:

Calories 405 | Fat 20g |Sodium 941mg | Carbs 26.1g | Fiber 0.9g | Sugar 0.9g | Protein 45.2g

Grilled Chicken Thighs with Pickled Peaches

Prep Time: 15 minutes.

Cook Time: 57 minutes.

Serves: 4

Ingredients:

Peaches

- 6 medium peaches
- 1 1/2 cups distilled white vinegar
- 1 cup sugar
- 1 stalk of lemongrass, sliced
- 1 (1-inch piece) ginger, peeled and sliced
- 1/2 teaspoon whole black peppercorns
- 5 allspice berries
- 2 whole cloves
- 1 (3-inch) cinnamon stick

Chicken

- 1 tablespoon sorghum syrup
- Kosher salt, to taste
- Black pepper, to taste
- 8 bone-in chicken thighs
- 1/2 cup 1 tablespoon olive oil
- 1 tablespoon red wine vinegar
- 2 garlic cloves, chopped
- 1/4 cup parsley, basil, and tarragon, chopped
- 4 cups arugula, thick stems discarded

Preparation:

1. Mix 8 cups water with 2 tbsp salt and sorghum syrup in a bowl

2. Add chicken to the sorghum water and cover to refrigerate overnight.

3. Remove the chicken to a bowl, then add garlic, herbs, 1 tsp pepper, vinegar, and ½ cup olive oil.

4. Place the chicken in the Ninja Foodi Smart XL grill.

5. Cover the Ninja Foodi Grill's hood, select the Manual Mode, set the temperature to 350 degrees F and grill on the "Grill Mode" for 25 minutes approximately.

6. Transfer the grilled chicken to a plate.

7. Add water to a saucepan and boil it.

8. Carve an X on top of the peaches and boil them in the water, then cook for 2 minutes.

9. Transfer the peaches to an ice bath, then peel the peaches.

10. Cut the peaches in half and remove the pit from the center.

11. Mix the rest of the ingredients for peaches and 1 ½ cups water in a saucepan.

12. Allow the glaze to cool, and toss in peaches.

13. Cover and refrigerate the peaches overnight.

14. Grill the peaches in the Ninja Foodi Smart XL grill for 10 minutes per side.

15. Serve the chicken and peaches with arugula.

16. Enjoy.

Serving Suggestion: Serve the peach chicken with a fresh crouton salad.

Variation Tip: Add a drizzle of cheese on top of the chicken after grilling.

Nutritional Information Per Serving:

Calories 545 | Fat 7.9g |Sodium 581mg | Carbs 41g | Fiber 2.6g | Sugar 0.1g | Protein 42.5g

Grilled Chicken with Grapes

Prep Time: 15 minutes.

Cook Time: 55 minutes.

Serves: 6

Ingredients:

- 1 cup whole buttermilk
- 1 cup water
- 1/2 cup yellow onion, sliced
- 2 tablespoons light brown sugar
- 1 1/2 tablespoons hot sauce
- 1 tablespoon salt
- 1 teaspoon black pepper
- 3 garlic cloves, smashed
- 3 boneless, skin-on chicken breasts
- 6 boneless, skin-on chicken thighs
- 1-pound Bronx grapes, separated into small clusters

Preparation:

1. Mix chicken with the rest of the ingredients except the grapes.
2. Cover and marinate the chicken for 30 minutes in the refrigerator.
3. Place the chicken in the Ninja Foodi Smart XL grill.
4. Cover the Ninja Foodi Grill's hood, select the Manual Mode, set the temperature to 350 degrees F and grill on the "Grill Mode" for 25 minutes approximately.
5. Flip the chicken once cooked halfway through.
6. Grill the grapes for 5-10 minutes per side until slightly charred.
7. Serve chicken with grilled grapes.
8. Enjoy.

Serving Suggestion: Serve the chicken with tomato sauce and toasted bread slices.

Variation Tip: Add butter sauce on top of the chicken before cooking.

Nutritional Information Per Serving:

Calories 419 | Fat 13g |Sodium 432mg | Carbs 9.1g | Fiber 3g | Sugar 1g | Protein 33g

Piri Piri Chicken

Prep Time: 15 minutes.

Cook Time: 8 minutes.

Serves: 2

Ingredients:

- 1 small red bell pepper, chopped
- 1/2 cup cilantro leaves
- 1 small shallot, chopped
- 2 tablespoons red wine vinegar
- 2 tablespoons olive oil
- 1 tablespoon paprika
- 2 garlic cloves, crushed
- 2 Piri Piri chiles stemmed
- 1 1/2 teaspoons dried oregano
- 1 tablespoon kosher salt
- 1 1/4 pounds chicken pieces
- Canola oil for brushing
- 1-pound Shishito peppers

Preparation:

1. Mix chicken piece with rest of the ingredients in a bowl.

2. Cover and refrigerate the chicken for 30 minutes for marination.

3. Place the chicken in the Ninja Foodi Smart XL grill.

4. Cover the Ninja Foodi Grill's hood, select the Manual Mode, set the temperature to 375 degrees F and grill on the "Grill Mode" for 8 minutes approximately.

5. Serve warm.

Serving Suggestion: Serve the chicken with roasted veggies on the side.

Variation Tip: Add sweet paprika for more taste.

Nutritional Information Per Serving:

Calories 334 | Fat 16g | Sodium 462mg | Carbs 31g | Fiber 0.4g | Sugar 3g | Protein 35.3g

Beef, Pork, and Lamb

Chili-Spiced Ribs

Prep Time: 15 minutes.

Cook Time: 50 minutes.

Serves: 6

Ingredients:

Glaze

- 1 cup of soy sauce
- 1 cup packed brown sugar
- 2/3 cup ketchup
- 1/3 cup lemon juice
- 1 ½ teaspoon fresh ginger root, minced

Ribs

- 6 lbs. pork baby back ribs
- 3 tablespoons packed brown sugar
- 2 tablespoons paprika
- 2 tablespoons chili powder
- 3 teaspoons ground cumin
- 2 teaspoons garlic powder
- 1 teaspoon salt

Preparation:

1. Take the first six ingredients in a suitable bowl and mix well.

2. Rub this mixture over the ribs, then covers them to refrigerate for 30 minutes of margination.

3. Place the ribs in the Ninja Foodi Smart XL grill.

4. Cover the Ninja Foodi Grill's hood, select the Manual Mode, set the temperature to 400 degrees F and grill on the "Grill Mode" for 45 minutes until al dente.

5. Flip the ribs after every 10 minutes for even cooking.

6. Meanwhile, prepare the sauce by cooking its ingredients for 8 minutes in a saucepan.

7. Pour this sauce over the grilled ribs in the Ninja Foodi Smart XL grill.

8. Grill for another 5 minutes side.

9. Serve.

Serving Suggestion: Serve the ribs with mashed potatoes.

Variation Tip: Use BBQ sauce for the change of taste.

Nutritional Information Per Serving:

Calories 305 | Fat 25g |Sodium 532mg | Carbs 2.3g | Fiber 0.4g | Sugar 2g | Protein 18.3g

Beef with Pesto

Prep Time: 15 minutes.

Cook Time: 14 minutes.

Serves: 2

Ingredients:

- 2 cups penne pasta, uncooked
- 2 (6 oz.) beef tenderloin steaks
- 1/4 teaspoon salt
- 1/4 teaspoon black pepper
- 5 oz. fresh baby spinach, chopped
- 2 cups grape tomatoes, halved
- 1/3 cup pesto
- ¼ cup walnuts, chopped
- 1/4 cup feta cheese, crumbled

Preparation:

1. At first, prepared the pasta as per the given instructions on the pack.
2. Drain and rinse, then keep this pasta aside.
3. Now season the tenderloin steaks with salt and black pepper.
4. Place the steaks in the Ninja Foodi Smart XL grill.
5. Cover the Ninja Foodi Grill's hood, select the Manual Mode, set the temperature to 375 degrees F and grill on the "Grill Mode" for 7 minutes.
6. Flip the steaks and continue grilling for another 7 minutes
7. Toss the pasta with spinach, tomatoes, walnuts, and pesto in a bowl.
8. Slice the grilled steak and top the salad with the steak.
9. Garnish with cheese.
10. Enjoy.

Serving Suggestion: Serve the beef with toasted bread slices.

Variation Tip: Add crumbled bacon to the mixture.

Nutritional Information Per Serving:

Calories 325 | Fat 16g |Sodium 431mg | Carbs 22g | Fiber 1.2g | Sugar 4g | Protein 23g

Sweet Chipotle Ribs

Prep Time: 15 minutes.

Cook Time: 20 minutes.

Serves: 8

Ingredients:

- 6 lbs. baby back ribs

Sauce

- 3 cups ketchup
- 2 (11.2 oz.) beer bottles
- 2 cups barbecue sauce
- 2/3 cup honey
- 1 small onion, chopped
- 1/4 cup Worcestershire sauce
- 2 tablespoons Dijon mustard
- 2 tablespoons chipotle in adobo sauce, chopped
- 4 teaspoons ground chipotle pepper
- 1 teaspoon salt
- 1 teaspoon garlic powder
- 1/2 teaspoon black pepper

Preparation:

1. First, wrap the ribs in a large foil and keep it aside.
2. Place the wrapped ribs in the Ninja Foodi Smart XL grill.
3. Cover the Ninja Foodi Grill's hood, select the Manual Mode, set the temperature to 375 degrees F and let it roast for 1 ½ hour.
4. Take the rest of the ingredients in a saucepan and cook for 45 minutes on a simmer.
5. Brush the grilled ribs with the prepared sauce generously.
6. Place the ribs back into the grill and continue grilling for 10 minutes per side.
7. Serve.

Serving Suggestion: Serve these ribs with rice, pasta, or spaghetti.

Variation Tip: Add maple syrup instead of honey.

Nutritional Information Per Serving:

Calories 425 | Fat 14g |Sodium 411mg | Carbs 44g | Fiber 0.3g | Sugar 1g | Protein 8.3g

Steak with Salsa Verde

Prep Time: 15 minutes.

Cook Time: 18 minutes.

Serves: 2

Ingredients:

- 1/4 teaspoon salt
- 1/4 teaspoon black pepper
- 1 cup salsa Verde
- 1/2 cup fresh cilantro leaves
- 1 ripe avocado, diced
- 1 beef flank steak, diced
- 1 medium tomato, seeded and diced

Preparation:

1. First, rub the steak with salt and pepper to season well.
2. Place the bread slices in the Ninja Foodi Smart XL grill.
3. Cover the Ninja Foodi Grill's hood, select the Manual Mode, set the temperature to 375 degrees F and grill on the "Grill Mode" for 9 minutes.
4. Flip and grill for another 9 minutes until al dente.
5. During this time, blend salsa with cilantro in a blender jug.
6. Slice the steak and serve it with salsa, tomato, and avocado.

Serving Suggestion: Serve the steak with sweet potato casserole.

Variation Tip: Add cheese on top of the steak and then bake after grilling.

Nutritional Information Per Serving:

Calories 425 | Fat 15g |Sodium 345mg | Carbs 12.3g | Fiber 1.4g | Sugar 3g | Protein 23.3g

Pork with Salsa

Prep Time: 15 minutes.

Cook Time: 12 minutes.

Serves: 4

Ingredients:

- 1/4 cup lime juice
- 2 tablespoons olive oil
- 2 garlic cloves, minced
- 1 ½ teaspoon ground cumin
- 1 ½ teaspoons dried oregano
- ½ teaspoon black pepper
- 2 lbs. pork tenderloin, ¾ inch slices

Salsa

- 1 jalapeno pepper, seeded and chopped
- 1/3 cup red onion, chopped
- 2 tablespoons fresh mint, chopped
- 2 tablespoons lime juice
- 4 cups pears, peeled and chopped
- 1 tablespoon lime zest, grated
- 1 teaspoon sugar
- 1/2 teaspoon black pepper

Preparation:

1. Season the pork with lime juice, cumin, oregano, oil, garlic, and pepper in a suitable bowl.
2. Cover to refrigerate for overnight margination.
3. Place the pork in the Ninja Foodi Smart XL grill.
4. Cover the Ninja Foodi Grill's hood, select the Manual Mode, set the temperature to 350 degrees F and grill on the "Grill Mode" for 6 minutes.
5. Flip the pork and continue grilling for another 6 minutes until al dente.
6. Mix the pear salsa ingredients into a separate bowl.
7. Serve the sliced pork with pear salsa.

Serving Suggestion: Serve the pork with mashed potatoes.

Variation Tip: Dust the pork chops with flour before grilling for more texture.

Nutritional Information Per Serving:

Calories 91 | Fat 5g |Sodium 88mg | Carbs 3g | Fiber 0g | Sugar 0g | Protein 7g

Ham Pineapple Skewers

Prep Time: 15 minutes.

Cook Time: 7 minutes.

Serves: 4

Ingredients:

- 1 can (20 oz.) pineapple chunks
- 1/2 cup orange marmalade
- 1 tablespoon mustard
- 1/4 teaspoon ground cloves
- 1 lb. ham, diced
- 1/2-lb. Swiss cheese, diced
- 1 medium green pepper, cubed

Preparation:

1. Take 2 tablespoons of pineapple from pineapples in a bowl.
2. Add mustard, marmalade, and cloves, mix well and keep it aside.
3. Thread the pineapple, green pepper, cheese, and ham over the skewers alternatively.
4. Place the ham skewers in the Ninja Foodi Smart XL grill.
5. Cover the Ninja Foodi Grill's hood, select the Manual Mode, set the temperature to 350 degrees F and grill on the "Grill Mode" for 7 minutes.
6. Continue rotating the skewers every 2 minutes.
7. Pour the sauce on top and serve.

Serving Suggestion: Serve the skewers with cream cheese dip.

Variation Tip: Serve the pineapple skewers on top of the fruit salad.

Nutritional Information Per Serving:

Calories 276 | Fat 21g |Sodium 476mg | Carbs 12g | Fiber 3g | Sugar 4g | Protein 10g

40. Steak Bread Salad

Prep Time: 15 minutes.

Cook Time: 8 minutes.

Serves: 2

Ingredients:

- 2 teaspoons chili powder
- 2 teaspoons brown sugar
- 1/2 teaspoon salt
- 1/2 teaspoon black pepper
- 1 beef top sirloin steak, diced
- 2 cups bread, cubed
- 2 tablespoons olive oil
- 1 cup ranch salad dressing
- 2 tablespoons horseradish, grated
- 1 tablespoon prepared mustard
- 3 large tomatoes, diced
- 1 medium cucumber, chopped
- 1 small red onion, thinly sliced

Preparation:

1. First, mix the chili powder with salt, pepper, and brown sugar in a bowl

2. Sauté the bread cubes with oil in a skillet for 10 minutes until golden.

3. Take a small bowl and mix horseradish with mustard and salad dressing.

4. Place the Steaks in the Ninja Foodi Smart XL grill.

5. Cover the Ninja Foodi Grill's hood, select the Manual Mode, set the temperature to 375 degrees F and grill on the "Grill Mode" for 4 minutes.

6. Flip the steak and continue grilling for another 4 minutes.

7. Toss the sautéed bread cubes with the rest of the ingredients and dressing mix in a salad bowl.

8. Slice the grilled steak and serve on top of the salad.

9. Enjoy.

Serving Suggestion: Serve the steak bread salad with crispy bacon on top.

Variation Tip: Grill bread cubes in the Ninja Foodi Smart XL grill for more texture.

Nutritional Information Per Serving:

Calories 380 | Fat 20g |Sodium 686mg | Carbs 33g | Fiber 1g | Sugar 1.2g | Protein 21g

Raspberry Pork Chops

Prep Time: 15 minutes.

Cook Time: 10 minutes.

Serves: 4

Ingredients:

- 1/2 cup seedless raspberry preserves
- 1 chipotle in adobo sauce, chopped
- 1/2 teaspoon salt
- 4 bone-in pork loin chops

Preparation:

1. Take a small pan and mix preserves with chipotle pepper sauce on medium heat.

2. Keep ¼ cup of this sauce aside and rub the remaining over the pork.

3. Sprinkle salt over the pork and mix well.

4. Place 2 pork chops in the Ninja Foodi Smart XL grill.

5. Cover the Ninja Foodi Grill's hood, select the Manual Mode, set the temperature to 400 degrees F and grill them on the "Grill Mode" for 5 minutes per side.

6. Grill the remaining chops in the same method.

7. Serve with the reserved sauce.

8. Enjoy.

Serving Suggestion: Serve the pork chops with boiled rice or spaghetti.

Variation Tip: Use apple sauce or maple syrup for seasoning.

Nutritional Information Per Serving:

Calories 361 | Fat 16g |Sodium 515mg | Carbs 19.3g | Fiber 0.1g | Sugar 18.2g | Protein 33.3g

Beef Cheese Burgers

Prep Time: 15 minutes.

Cook Time: 20 minutes.

Serves: 4

Ingredients:

- 1/2 cup shredded cheddar cheese
- 6 tablespoons chili sauce, divided
- 1 tablespoon chili powder
- 1-lb. ground beef

To serve

- 4 hamburger buns, split
- Lettuce leaves, tomato slices, and mayonnaise,

Preparation:

1. First, take all the ingredients for patties in a bowl.
2. Thoroughly mix them together, then make 4 of the ½ inch patties out of it.
3. Place 2 patties in the Ninja Foodi Smart XL grill.
4. Cover the Ninja Foodi Grill's hood, select the Manual Mode, set the temperature to 350 degrees F and grill them on the "Grill Mode" for 5 minutes per side.
5. Grill the remaining patties in a similar way.
6. Serve with buns, lettuce, tomato, and mayonnaise.

Serving Suggestion: Serve the beef cheeseburgers with mayo dip.

Variation Tip: Add butter to the patties before cooking.

Nutritional Information Per Serving:

Calories 405 | Fat 22.7g |Sodium 227mg | Carbs 26.1g | Fiber 1.4g | Sugar 0.9g | Protein 45.2g

Bratwurst Potatoes

Prep Time: 15 minutes.

Cook Time: 25 minutes.

Serves: 6

Ingredients:

- 3 lbs. bratwurst links, uncooked
- 3 lbs. small red potatoes, wedged
- 1-lb. baby carrots
- 1 large red onion, sliced and rings
- 2 jars (4-1/2 oz.) whole mushrooms, drained
- 1/4 cup butter, cubed
- 1 pack onion soup mix
- 2 tablespoons soy sauce
- 1/2 teaspoon black pepper

Preparation:

1. Place 2 foil packets on the working surface.
2. Divide the potatoes, carrots, onion, brats, and mushrooms with the foil.
3. Top them with butter, soup mix, pepper, and soy sauce.
4. Seal the foil packets by pinching their ends together.
5. Place one foil packet in the Ninja Foodi Smart XL grill.
6. Cover the Ninja Foodi Grill's hood, select the Manual Mode, set the temperature to 375 degrees F and grill on the "Grill Mode" for 25 minutes.
7. Cook the other half of the brat's mixture in a similar way.
8. Open the packets carefully and be careful of the steam.
9. Serve.

Serving Suggestion: Serve the bratwurst potatoes with boiled peas, carrots, and potatoes on the side.

Variation Tip: Add butter to the potatoes for more taste.

Nutritional Information Per Serving:

Calories 345 | Fat 36g |Sodium 272mg | Carbs 41g | Fiber 0.2g | Sugar 0.1g | Protein 22.5g

Crusted Beef Burger

Prep Time: 15 minutes.

Cook Time: 10 minutes.

Serves: 4

Ingredients:

- 1/2 cup seasoned bread crumbs
- 1 large egg, lightly beaten
- 1/2 teaspoon salt
- 1/2 teaspoon black pepper
- 1-lb. ground beef
- 1 tablespoon olive oil
- 4 sesame seed hamburger buns, split

Preparation:

1. Take all the ingredients for a burger in a suitable bowl except the oil and the buns.
2. Mix them thoroughly together and make 4 of the ½ inch patties.
3. Brush these patties with olive oil.
4. Place 2 patties in the Ninja Foodi Smart XL grill.
5. Cover the Ninja Foodi Grill's hood, select the Manual Mode, set the temperature to 375 degrees F and grill them on the "Grill Mode" for 5 minutes per side until al dente.
6. Grill the remaining two patties in the same way.
7. Serve with buns.

Serving Suggestion: Serve the burgers with sautéed green beans and mashed potatoes.

Variation Tip: Insert a cheese cube to the center of each patty.

Nutritional Information Per Serving:

Calories 395 | Fat 9.5g |Sodium 655mg | Carbs 13.4g | Fiber 0.4g | Sugar 0.4g | Protein 28.3g

Beef Chimichurri Skewers

Prep Time: 15 minutes.

Cook Time: 10 minutes.

Serves: 4

Ingredients:

- 1/3 cup fresh basil
- 1/3 cup fresh cilantro
- 1/3 cup fresh parsley
- 1 tablespoon red wine vinegar
- Juice of 1/2 lemon
- 1 Garlic clove, minced
- 1 shallot, minced
- 1/2 teaspoon crushed red pepper flakes
- 1/2 cup olive oil, divided
- Salt to taste
- Black pepper to taste
- 1 red onion, cubed
- 1 red pepper, cubed
- 1 orange pepper, cubed
- 1 yellow pepper, cubed
- 1 1/2 lb. sirloin steak, fat trimmed and diced

Preparation:

1. First, take basil, parsley, vinegar, lemon juice, red pepper, shallots, garlic, and cilantro in a blender jug.
2. Blend well, then add ¼ cup olive oil, salt, and pepper and mix again.
3. Now thread the steak, peppers, and onion on the skewers.
4. Drizzle salt, black pepper, and remaining oil over the skewers.
5. Place four skewers in the Ninja Foodi Smart XL grill.
6. Cover the Ninja Foodi Grill's hood, select the Manual Mode, set the temperature to 375 degrees F and grill them on the "Grill Mode" for 5 minutes per side.
7. Grill the skewers in a batch until all are cooked.
8. Serve warm with green sauce.

Serving Suggestion: Serve the skewers with fresh green and mashed potatoes.

Variation Tip: Add a drizzle of herbs on top of the skewers.

Nutritional Information Per Serving:

Calories 301 | Fat 5g |Sodium 340mg | Carbs 24.7g | Fiber 1.2g | Sugar 1.3g | Protein 15.3g

Lamb Skewers

Prep Time: 15 minutes.

Cook Time: 8 minutes.

Serves: 4

Ingredients:

- 1 (10 oz.) pack couscous
- 1 ½ cup yogurt
- 1 tablespoon 1 teaspoon cumin
- 2 garlic cloves, minced
- Juice of 2 lemons
- Salt to taste
- Black pepper to taste
- 1 1/2 lb. leg of lamb, boneless, diced
- 2 tomatoes, seeded and diced
- 1/2 English cucumber, seeded and diced
- 1/2 small red onion, chopped
- 1/4 cup fresh parsley, chopped
- 1/4 cup fresh mint, chopped
- 3 tablespoon olive oil
- Lemon wedges, for serving

Preparation:

1. First, cook the couscous as per the given instructions on the package, then fluff with a fork.
2. Whisk yogurt with garlic, cumin, lemon juice, salt, and black pepper in a large bowl.
3. Add lamb and mix well to coat the meat.
4. Separately toss red onion with cucumber, tomatoes, parsley, mint, lemon juice, olive oil, salt, and couscous in a salad bowl.
5. Thread the seasoned lamb on 8 skewers and drizzle salt and black pepper over them.
6. Place 4 lamb skewers in the Ninja Foodi Smart XL grill.
7. Cover the Ninja Foodi Grill's hood, select the Manual Mode, set the temperature to 400 degrees F and grill them on the "Grill Mode" for 4 minutes per side.
8. Cook the remaining skewers in a similar way.
9. Serve warm with prepared couscous.

Serving Suggestion: Serve the lamb skewers with quinoa salad.

Variation Tip: Add barbecue sauce to the lamb cube skewers.

Nutritional Information Per Serving:

Calories 448 | Fat 23g |Sodium 350mg | Carbs 18g | Fiber 6.3g | Sugar 1g | Protein 40.3g

Korean Beef Steak

Prep Time: 15 minutes.

Cook Time: 12 minutes.

Serves: 2

Ingredients:

- 1/2 cup 1 tablespoon soy sauce
- 1/4 cup 2 tablespoon vegetable oil
- 1/2 cup rice wine vinegar
- 4 garlic cloves, minced
- 2 tablespoon ginger, minced
- 2 tablespoon honey
- 3 tablespoon sesame oil
- 3 tablespoon Sriracha
- 1 1/2 lb. flank steak
- 1 teaspoon sugar
- 1 teaspoon crushed red pepper flakes
- 2 cucumbers, cut lengthwise, seeded and sliced
- Salt to taste

Preparation:

1. Mix ½ cup soy sauce, half of the rice wine, honey, ginger, garlic, 2 tablespoon Sriracha sauce, 2 tablespoon sesame oil, and vegetable oil in a large bowl.
2. Pour half of this sauce over the steak and rub it well.
3. Cover the steak and marinate for 10 minutes.
4. For the salad, mix remaining rice wine vinegar, sesame oil, sugar, red pepper flakes, Sriracha sauce, soy sauce, and salt in a salad bowl.
5. Place the steak in the Ninja Foodi Smart XL grill.
6. Cover the Ninja Foodi Grill's hood, select the Manual Mode, set the temperature to 375 degrees F and grill on the "Grill Mode" for 6 minutes per side.
7. Slice and serve with cucumber salad.

Serving Suggestion: Serve the flank steak with sautéed vegetables and toasted bread slices.

Variation Tip: Use maple syrup instead of honey for a unique sweet taste.

Nutritional Information Per Serving:

Calories 309 | Fat 25g | Sodium 463mg | Carbs 9.9g | Fiber 0.3g | Sugar 0.3g | Protein 18g

Fajita Skewers

Prep Time: 15 minutes.

Cook Time: 7 minutes.

Serves: 4

Ingredients:

- 1 lb. sirloin steak, cubed
- 1 bunch scallions, cut into large pieces
- 1 pack flour tortillas, torn
- 4 large bell peppers, cubed
- 8 skewers
- Olive oil, for drizzling
- Salt to taste
- Black pepper to taste

Preparation:

1. Thread the steak, tortillas, peppers, and scallions on the skewers.
2. Drizzle salt, black pepper, and olive oil over the skewers.
3. Place 4 skewers in the Ninja Foodi Smart XL grill.
4. Cover the Ninja Foodi Grill's hood, select the Manual Mode, set the temperature to 400 degrees F and grill them on the "Grill Mode" for 7 minutes.
5. Continue rotating the skewers every 2 minutes.
6. Cook the skewers in batches until all are grilled.
7. Serve warm.

Serving Suggestion: Serve the fajita skewers with mashed potatoes.

Variation Tip: Add more veggies of your choice to the skewers.

Nutritional Information Per Serving:

Calories 537 | Fat 20g |Sodium 719mg | Carbs 25.1g | Fiber 0.9g | Sugar 1.4g | Protein 37.8g

Fish and Seafood

Shrimp with Tomatoes

Prep Time: 15 minutes.

Cook Time: 8 minutes.

Serves: 6

Ingredients:

- 2/3 cup fresh arugula
- 1/3 cup lemon juice
- 2 tablespoons olive oil
- 2 garlic cloves, minced
- 1/2 teaspoon grated lemon zest
- 1-lb. uncooked shrimp, peeled and deveined
- 2 green onions, sliced
- 1/4 cup plain yogurt
- 2 teaspoons 2% milk
- 1 teaspoon cider vinegar
- 1 teaspoon Dijon mustard
- 1/2 teaspoon sugar
- 1/2 teaspoon salt, divided
- 12 cherry tomatoes
- 1/4 teaspoon black pepper

Preparation:

1. Season the shrimp with lemon juice, lemon zest, oil, and garlic in a suitable bowl.
2. Let it for 10 minutes of margination.
3. Now arugula, yogurt, milk, green onion, sugar, vinegar, mustard, and ¼ teaspoon salt in a blender.
4. Thread the seasoned shrimp and tomatoes on the skewers alternately.
5. And season the skewers with salt and black pepper.
6. Place the skewers in the Ninja Foodi Smart XL grill.
7. Cover the Ninja Foodi Grill's hood, select the Manual Mode, set the temperature to 325 degrees F and let them grill on the "Grill Mode" for 2 minutes per side.
8. Cook the shrimp in batches.

9.   Serve with the prepared sauce.

Serving Suggestion: Serve the shrimp tomatoes meal on top of the rice risotto.

Variation Tip: Add paprika for more spice.

Nutritional Information Per Serving:

Calories 448 | Fat 13g |Sodium 353mg | Carbs 31g | Fiber 0.4g | Sugar 1g | Protein 29g

Ginger Salmon

Prep Time: 15 minutes.

Cook Time: 8 minutes.

Serves: 10

Ingredients:

- 2 tablespoons rice vinegar
- 4 teaspoons sugar
- 1/2 teaspoon salt
- 1 tablespoon lime zest, grated
- 1/4 cup lime juice
- 2 tablespoons olive oil
- 1/2 teaspoon ground coriander
- 1/2 teaspoon black pepper
- 1/3 cup fresh cilantro, chopped
- 1 tablespoon onion, chopped
- 2 teaspoons fresh ginger root, minced
- 2 garlic cloves, minced
- 2 medium cucumbers, peeled, seeded, and chopped

SALMON

- 1/3 cup minced fresh gingerroot
- 1 tablespoon lime juice
- 1 tablespoon olive oil
- 1/2 teaspoon salt
- 1/2 teaspoon freshly ground pepper
- 10 (6 oz.) salmon fillets

Preparation:

1. Start by blending the first 13 ingredients in a blender until smooth.
2. Season the salmon fillets with ginger, oil, salt, black pepper, lime juice.
3. Place 2 salmon fillets in the Ninja Foodi Smart XL grill.
4. Cover the Ninja Foodi Grill's hood, select the Manual Mode, set the temperature to 350 degrees F and grill them on the "Grill Mode" for 4 minutes per side.
5. Cook the remaining fillets in a similar way.
6. Serve with the prepared sauce.

Serving Suggestion: Serve the ginger salmon with crispy onion rings on the side.

Variation Tip: Add honey for seasoning.

Nutritional Information Per Serving:

Calories 376 | Fat 17g |Sodium 1127mg | Carbs 24g | Fiber 1g | Sugar 3g | Protein 29g

Pistachio Pesto Shrimp

Prep Time: 15 minutes.

Cook Time: 6 minutes.

Serves: 4

Ingredients:

- 3/4 cup fresh arugula
- 1/2 cup parsley, minced
- 1/3 cup shelled pistachios
- 2 tablespoons lemon juice
- 1 garlic clove, peeled
- 1/4 teaspoon lemon zest, grated
- 1/2 cup olive oil
- 1/4 cup Parmesan cheese, shredded
- 1/4 teaspoon salt
- 1/8 teaspoon black pepper
- 1-1/2 lbs. jumbo shrimp, peeled and deveined

Preparation:

1. Start by adding the first 6 ingredients in a blender until smooth.
2. Add salt, pepper, Parmesan cheese, and mix well.
3. Toss in shrimp and mix well, then cover to refrigerate for 30 minutes.
4. Thread these shrimps on the skewers.
5. Place the skewers in the Ninja Foodi Smart XL grill.
6. Cover the Ninja Foodi Grill's hood, select the Manual Mode, set the temperature to 325 degrees F and grill them on the "Grill Mode" for 6 minutes.
7. Continue rotating skewers after every 2 minutes.
8. Cook the skewers in batches.
9. Serve.

Serving Suggestion: Serve the pesto shrimp with fresh greens and chili sauce on the side.

Variation Tip: Roll the shrimp in breadcrumbs for a crispy touch.

Nutritional Information Per Serving:

Calories 457 | Fat 19g |Sodium 557mg | Carbs 19g | Fiber 1.8g | Sugar 1.2g | Protein 32.5g

Lemon-Garlic Salmon

Prep Time: 15 minutes.

Cook Time: 9 minutes.

Serves: 4

Ingredients:

- 2 garlic cloves, minced
- 2 teaspoons lemon zest, grated
- 1/2 teaspoon salt
- 1/2 teaspoon fresh rosemary, minced
- 1/2 teaspoon black pepper
- 4 (6 oz.) salmon fillets

Preparation:

1. Take the first five ingredients in a bowl and mix well.
2. Leave the mixture for 15 minutes, then rub the salmon with this mixture.
3. Place 2 salmon fillets in the Ninja Foodi Smart XL grill.
4. Cover the Ninja Foodi Grill's hood, select the Manual Mode, set the temperature to 350 degrees F and grill them on the "Grill Mode" for 6 minutes.
5. Flip the salmon fillets after 3 minutes.
6. Serve warm.

Serving Suggestion: Serve the lemon garlic salmon with butter sauce on top.

Variation Tip: Grill the veggies on the side to serve with the salmon.

Nutritional Information Per Serving:

Calories 392 | Fat 16g |Sodium 466mg | Carbs 3.9g | Fiber 0.9g | Sugar 0.6g | Protein 48g

Shrimp Stuffed Sole

Prep Time: 15 minutes.

Cook Time: 14 minutes.

Serves: 4

Ingredients:

- 1/4 cup soft bread crumbs
- 1/4 cup butter, melted
- 2 tablespoons whipped cream cheese
- 2 teaspoons chives, minced
- 1 garlic clove, minced
- 1 teaspoon lemon zest, grated
- 1 can (6 oz.) crabmeat, drained
- 1 teaspoon parsley, minced
- 4 sole fillets (6 oz.), cut from a side and insides removed
- 1/2 cup shrimp, cooked, peeled, and chopped
- 1-1/2 cups cherry tomatoes
- 2 tablespoons chicken broth
- 2 tablespoons lemon juice
- 1/2 teaspoon salt
- 1/2 teaspoon black pepper

Preparation:

1. Thoroughly mix crab with shrimp, cream cheese, chives, lemon zest, garlic, parsley, 2 tablespoon butter, and breadcrumbs in a small bowl.
2. Stuff ¼ of this filling into each fillet and secure the ends by inserting the toothpicks.
3. Mix tomatoes with salt, pepper, wine, and lemon juice in a separate bowl.
4. Place each stuffed fillet in a foil sheet and top with tomato mixture.
5. Cover and seal the fillets in the foil.
6. Place 2 sealed fillets in the Ninja Foodi Smart XL grill.
7. Cover the Ninja Foodi Grill's hood, select the Manual Mode, set the temperature to 350 degrees F and cook them on the "Bake Mode" for 7 minutes per side.
8. Cook the remaining fillets in a similar way.
9. Serve warm.

Serving Suggestion: Serve the shrimp stuffed with the sole with fried rice.

Variation Tip: Serve the sole fish with breadcrumbs and butter sauce on top.

Nutritional Information Per Serving:

Calories 321 | Fat 7.4g |Sodium 356mg | Carbs 9.3g | Fiber 2.4g | Sugar 5g | Protein 37.2g

Salmon Lime Burgers

Prep Time: 15 minutes.

Cook Time: 20 minutes.

Serves: 4

Ingredients:

- 1-lb. salmon fillets, cubed
- 2 tablespoons grated lime zest
- 1 tablespoon Dijon mustard
- 3 tablespoons shallot, chopped
- 2 tablespoons fresh cilantro, minced
- 1 tablespoon soy sauce
- 1 tablespoon honey
- 3 garlic cloves, minced
- 1/2 teaspoon salt
- 1/4 teaspoon black pepper
- 4 hamburger buns, split

Preparation:

1. Thoroughly mix all the ingredients for burgers in a bowl except the buns.
2. Make four of the ½ patties out of this mixture.
3. Place 2 patties in the Ninja Foodi Smart XL grill.
4. Cover the Ninja Foodi Grill's hood, select the Manual Mode, set the temperature to 350 degrees F and grill them on the "Grill Mode" for 5 minutes per side.
5. Grill the remaining patties in a similar way.
6. Serve warm with buns.

Serving Suggestion: Serve the salmon lime burgers with vegetable rice.

Variation Tip: Add canned corn to the burgers.

Nutritional Information Per Serving:

Calories 258 | Fat 9g |Sodium 994mg | Carbs 1g | Fiber 0.4g | Sugar 3g | Protein 16g

Salmon Packets

Prep Time: 15 minutes.

Cook Time: 10 minutes.

Serves: 4

Ingredients:

- 4 (6 oz.) salmon steaks
- 1 teaspoon lemon-pepper seasoning
- 1 cup shredded carrots
- 1/2 cup julienned sweet yellow pepper
- 1/2 cup julienned green pepper
- 4 teaspoons lemon juice
- 1 teaspoon dried parsley flakes
- 1/2 teaspoon salt
- 1/4 teaspoon black pepper

Preparation:

1.   Season the salmon with lemon pepper, then place it on a 12-inch square foil sheet.

2.   Top the salmon with the remaining ingredients, then seal the foil.

3.   Place 2 fish pockets in the Ninja Foodi Smart XL grill.

4.   Cover the Ninja Foodi Grill's hood, select the Manual Mode, set the temperature to 375 degrees F and cook on the "bake Mode" for 5 minutes per side.

5.   Cook the remaining fillets in a similar way.

6.   Serve warm.

Serving Suggestion: Serve the salmon packets with lemon slices and fried rice.

Variation Tip: Use herbs to the seafood for a change of flavor.

Nutritional Information Per Serving:

Calories 378 | Fat 21g | Sodium 146mg | Carbs 7.1g | Fiber 0.1g | Sugar 0.4g | Protein 23g

Blackened Salmon

Prep Time: 15 minutes.

Cook Time: 20 minutes.

Serves: 2

Ingredients:

- 1 lb. salmon fillets
- 3 tablespoons melted butter
- 1 tablespoon lemon pepper
- 1 teaspoon seasoned salt
- 1½ tablespoon smoked paprika
- 1 teaspoon cayenne pepper
- ¾ teaspoon onion salt
- ½ teaspoon dry basil
- ½ teaspoon ground white pepper
- ½ teaspoon ground black pepper
- ¼ teaspoon dry oregano
- ¼ teaspoon ancho chili powder
- olive oil cooking spray
- fresh dill sprigs, to serve
- lemon wedges

Preparation:

1. Liberally season the salmon fillets with butter and other ingredients.
2. Place the fish pockets in the Ninja Foodi Smart XL grill.
3. Cover the Ninja Foodi Grill's hood, select the Manual Mode, set the temperature to 350 degrees F and cook on the "Bake Mode" for 10 minutes per side.
4. Serve warm.

Serving Suggestion: Serve the blackened salmon with fresh greens.

Variation Tip: Drizzle lemon juice on top for a rich taste.

Nutritional Information Per Serving:

Calories 351 | Fat 4g |Sodium 236mg | Carbs 19.1g | Fiber 0.3g | Sugar 0.1g | Protein 36g

Citrus-Soy Squid

Prep Time: 15 minutes.

Cook Time: 6 minutes.

Serves: 6

Ingredients:

- 1 cup mirin
- 1 cup soy sauce
- 1/3 cup yuzu juice
- 2 pounds squid tentacles, cut crosswise 1 inch thick

Preparation:

1. Toss squid with mirin, soy sauce, and water yuzu juice in a bowl.
2. Cover and marinate the squid for 4 hours in the refrigerator.
3. Place the squids in the Ninja Foodi Smart XL grill.
4. Cover the Ninja Foodi Grill's hood, select the Manual Mode, set the temperature to 300 degrees F and grill them on the "Grill Mode" for 3 minutes per side.
5. Serve warm.

Serving Suggestion: Serve the grilled squid with mashed potatoes.

Variation Tip: Coat the squid with breadcrumbs.

Nutritional Information Per Serving:

Calories 378 | Fat 7g |Sodium 316mg | Carbs 16.2g | Fiber 0.3g | Sugar 0.3g | Protein 26g

Clams with Horseradish-Tabasco Sauce

Prep Time: 15 minutes.

Cook Time: 4 minutes.

Serves: 6

Ingredients:

- 4 tablespoons unsalted butter, softened
- 2 tablespoons drained horseradish
- 1 tablespoon Tabasco
- 1/4 teaspoon lemon zest, grated
- 1 tablespoon fresh lemon juice
- 1/4 teaspoon Spanish smoked paprika
- Salt, to taste
- 2 dozen littleneck clams, scrubbed
- Grilled slices of crusty white bread for serving

Preparation:

1. Blend butter with lemon zest, Tabasco, lemon juice, pimento de la Vera, salt, and horseradish in a small bowl.
2. Place the clams in the Ninja Foodi Smart XL grill.
3. Cover the Ninja Foodi Grill's hood, select the Manual Mode, set the temperature to 325 degrees F and grill them on the "Grill Mode" for 2 minutes per side.
4. Serve the clams with a horseradish mixture.

Serving Suggestion: Serve the clams with roasted broccoli florets.

Variation Tip: Drizzle lemon garlic butter on top before cooking.

Nutritional Information Per Serving:
Calories 415 | Fat 15g |Sodium 634mg | Carbs 14.3g | Fiber 1.4g | Sugar 1g | Protein 23.3g

Grilled Shrimp with Miso Butter

Prep Time: 15 minutes.

Cook Time: 8 minutes.

Serves: 6

Ingredients:

- 1 stick unsalted butter, softened
- 2 tablespoons white miso
- 1/2 teaspoon lemon zest, grated
- 1 tablespoon lemon juice
- 1 tablespoon scallion, sliced
- 1-pound large shrimp, shelled and deveined
- 2 tablespoons canola oil
- 1 large garlic clove, minced
- 1 teaspoon Korean chile powder
- 1 teaspoon salt
- 1 1/2 teaspoons mustard seeds, pickled

Preparation:

1. Blend butter with lemon juice, lemon zest, miso, 1 tablespoon scallion in a bowl.
2. Toss in shrimp, chile powder, salt, and garlic, then mix well.
3. Place shrimps in the Ninja Foodi Smart XL grill.
4. Cover the Ninja Foodi Grill's hood, select the Manual Mode, set the temperature to 325 degrees F and grill them on the "Grill Mode" for 4 minutes per side.
5. Serve warm.

Serving Suggestion: Serve the shrimp with potato salad.

Variation Tip: Add garlic salt to the sauce for more taste.

Nutritional Information Per Serving:

Calories 251 | Fat 17g |Sodium 723mg | Carbs 21g | Fiber 2.5g | Sugar 2g | Protein 7.3g

Vegetables and Sides

Vegetable Orzo Salad

Prep Time: 15 minutes.

Cook Time: 14 minutes.

Serves: 4

Ingredients:

- 1-1/4 cups orzo, uncooked
- 1/2-lb. fresh asparagus, trimmed
- 1 zucchini, sliced
- 1 sweet yellow, halved
- 1 portobello mushroom, stem removed
- 1/2 red onion, halved

Salad

- 1/2 teaspoon salt
- 1 cup grape tomatoes, halved
- 1 tablespoon minced fresh parsley
- 1 tablespoon minced fresh basil
- 1/4 teaspoon black pepper
- 1 cup (4 oz.) feta cheese, crumbled

Dressing

- 4 garlic cloves, minced
- 1/3 cup olive oil
- 1/4 cup balsamic vinegar
- 3 tablespoons lemon juice
- 1 teaspoon lemon-pepper seasoning

Preparation:

1. Cook the orzo as per the given instructions on the package, then drain.
2. Toss all the salad and dressing ingredients in a bowl until well coated.
3. Place the mushrooms, pepper, and onion in the Ninja Foodi Smart XL grill.

4. Cover the Ninja Foodi Grill's hood, select the Manual Mode, set the temperature to 325 degrees F and grill them on the "Grill Mode" for 5 minutes per side.

5. Now grill zucchini and asparagus for 2 minutes per side.

6. Dice the grilled veggies and add them to the salad bowl.

7. Mix well, then stir in orzo.

8. Give it a toss, then serve.

Serving Suggestion: Serve the orzo salad with guacamole on top.

Variation Tip: Add olives or sliced mushrooms to the salad.

Nutritional Information Per Serving:

Calories 246 | Fat 15g |Sodium 220mg | Carbs 40.3g | Fiber 2.4g | Sugar 1.2g | Protein 12.4g

Southwestern Potato Salad

Prep Time: 15 minutes.

Cook Time: 14 minutes.

Serves: 6

Ingredients:

- 1-1/2 lbs. large red potatoes quartered lengthwise
- 3 tablespoons olive oil
- 2 poblano peppers
- 2 medium ears sweet corn, husks removed
- 1/2 cup buttermilk
- 1/2 cup sour cream
- 1 tablespoon lime juice
- 1 jalapeno pepper, seeded and minced
- 1 tablespoon minced fresh cilantro
- 1-1/2 teaspoons garlic salt
- 1 teaspoon ground cumin
- 1/4 teaspoon cayenne pepper

Preparation:

1. Add water and potatoes to a large saucepan and cook for 5 minutes on a boil.
2. Drain and rub the potatoes with oil.
3. Place the poblanos in the Ninja Foodi Smart XL grill.
4. Cover the Ninja Foodi Grill's hood, select the Manual Mode, set the temperature to 350 degrees F and grill on the "Grill Mode" for 5 minutes per side.
5. Now grill potatoes and corn for 7 minutes per side.
6. Peel the pepper and chop them.
7. Cut corn and potatoes as well and mix well peppers in a bowl.
8. Whisk the rest of the ingredients in a separate bowl, then add to the potatoes.
9. Mix well and serve.

Serving Suggestion: Serve the potato salad with pita bread.

Variation Tip: Add boiled chickpeas to the salad

Nutritional Information Per Serving:

Calories 338 | Fat 24g |Sodium 620mg | Carbs 58.3g | Fiber 2.4g | Sugar 1.2g | Protein 5.4g

Apple Salad

Prep Time: 15 minutes.

Cook Time: 10 minutes.

Serves: 4

Ingredients:

- 6 tablespoons olive oil
- 1/4 cup cilantro, minced
- 1/4 cup vinegar
- 2 tablespoons honey
- 1 garlic clove, minced
- 1/4 cup orange juice
- 1/2 teaspoon salt
- 1/2 teaspoon Sriracha chili sauce
- 2 large apples, wedged
- 1 pack (5 oz.) salad greens
- 1 cup walnut halves, toasted
- 1/2 cup crumbled blue cheese

Preparation:

1. Whisk the first 8 ingredients in a bowl and add ¼ cup of this dressing to the apples.
2. Toss well and let them sit for 10 minutes.
3. Place the apples in the Ninja Foodi Smart XL grill.
4. Cover the Ninja Foodi Grill's hood, select the Manual Mode, set the temperature to 325 degrees F and grill on the "Grill Mode" for 5 minutes per side.
5. Toss the rest of the salad ingredients together in a salad bowl.
6. Add grilled apples and serve.

Serving Suggestion: Serve the apple salad with lemon wedges.

Variation Tip: Add breadcrumbs to the salad for a crispy texture.

Nutritional Information Per Serving:

Calories 93 | Fat 3g |Sodium 510mg | Carbs 12g | Fiber 3g | Sugar 4g | Protein 4g

Potatoes in a Foil

Prep Time: 15 minutes.

Cook Time: 25 minutes.

Serves: 4

Ingredients:

- 2 ½ lbs. potatoes, peeled and diced
- 1 medium onion, chopped
- 5 bacon strips, cooked and crumbled
- 1/4 cup butter, melted
- 1/2 teaspoon salt
- 1/4 teaspoon black pepper
- 6 slices American cheese
- Sour cream, to serve

Preparation:

1. Toss potatoes with salt, pepper, butter, bacon, and onion.
2. Add this mixture to a suitably sized foil sheet and wrap it well to seal.
3. Place the potato pockets in the Ninja Foodi Smart XL grill.
4. Cover the Ninja Foodi Grill's hood, select the Manual Mode, set the temperature to 350 degrees F and cook on the "Bake Mode" for 25 minutes.
5. Drizzle cheese over hot potatoes.
6. Serve warm.

Serving Suggestion: Serve the potatoes with butter sauce and bacon on top.

Variation Tip: Add boiled green beans to the potatoes before serving.

Nutritional Information Per Serving:

Calories 378 | Fat 3.8g |Sodium 620mg | Carbs 13.3g | Fiber 2.4g | Sugar 1.2g | Protein 5.4g

Cajun Green Beans

Prep Time: 15 minutes.

Cook Time: 11 minutes.

Serves: 4

Ingredients:

- 1-lb. fresh green beans, trimmed
- 1/2 teaspoon Cajun seasoning
- 1 tablespoon butter

Preparation:

1. Add green beans to an 18-inch square sheet.
2. Drizzle Cajun seasoning and butter on top.
3. Cover and seal the foil over the green beans.
4. Place the green bean pockets in the Ninja Foodi Smart XL grill.
5. Cover the Ninja Foodi Grill's hood, select the Manual Mode, set the temperature to 350 degrees F and cook on the "Bake Mode" for 11 minutes.
6. Serve warm

Serving Suggestion: Serve the green beans with crispy nachos and mashed potatoes.

Variation Tip: Add crispy dried onion for better taste.

Nutritional Information Per Serving:

Calories 304 | Fat 31g |Sodium 834mg | Carbs 21.4g | Fiber 0.2g | Sugar 0.3g | Protein 4.6g

Grilled Veggies with Vinaigrette

Prep Time: 15 minutes.

Cook Time: 16 minutes.

Serves: 4

Ingredients:

Vinaigrette

- 1/4 cup red wine vinegar
- 1 tablespoon Dijon mustard
- 1 tablespoon honey
- 1/2 teaspoon salt
- 1/8 teaspoon black pepper
- 1/4 cup canola oil
- 1/4 cup olive oil

Vegetables

- 2 large sweet onions, diced
- 2 medium zucchinis, diced
- 2 yellow summer squash, diced
- 2 red peppers, seeded and cut in half
- 1 bunch green onions, trimmed
- Cooking spray

Preparation:

1. Start by whisking the first 5 ingredients in a small bowl.
2. Gradually add oil while mixing the vinaigrette thoroughly.
3. Place the onion quarters in the Ninja Foodi Smart XL grill.
4. Cover the Ninja Foodi Grill's hood, select the Manual Mode, set the temperature to 350 degrees F and grill on the "Grill Mode" for 5 minutes per side.
5. Grill squash, peppers, and zucchini for 7 minutes per side in the same grill.
6. Finally, grill the green onions for 1 minute per side.
7. Dice the grilled veggies and mix with vinaigrette.
8. Serve.

Serving Suggestion: Serve the vegetables with boiled rice or pasta.

Variation Tip: Top the veggies with feta cheese before serving.

Nutritional Information Per Serving:

Calories 341 | Fat 24g |Sodium 547mg | Carbs 36.4g | Fiber 1.2g | Sugar 1g | Protein 10.3g

Grilled Potato Rounds

Prep Time: 15 minutes.

Cook Time: 14 minutes.

Serves: 4

Ingredients:

- 4 large potatoes, baked and cooled
- 1/4 cup butter, melted
- 1/4 teaspoon salt
- 1/4 teaspoon black pepper
- 1 cup sour cream
- 1-1/2 cups cheddar cheese, shredded
- 8 bacon strips, cooked and crumbled
- 3 tablespoons chives, minced

Preparation:

1. First, cut the potatoes into 1-inch thick rounds.
2. Rub them with butter, salt, and black pepper.
3. Place the potatoes slices in the Ninja Foodi Smart XL grill.
4. Cover the Ninja Foodi Grill's hood, select the Manual Mode, set the temperature to 350 degrees F and grill on the "Grill Mode" for 7 minutes per side.
5. Serve warm with bacon, chives, cheese and sour cream on top.
6. Enjoy.

Serving Suggestion: Serve the potatoes with tomato sauce.

Variation Tip: Add green beans around the potatoes before serving.

Nutritional Information Per Serving:

Calories 318 | Fat 15.7g |Sodium 124mg | Carbs 27g | Fiber 0.1g | Sugar 0.3g | Protein 4.9g

Grilled Cauliflower with Miso Mayo

Prep Time: 15 minutes.

Cook Time: 20 minutes.

Serves: 6

Ingredients:

- 1 head of cauliflower, cut into florets
- 1/2 teaspoons kosher salt
- 4 tablespoons unsalted butter
- 1/4 cup hot sauce
- 1 tablespoon ketchup
- 1 tablespoon soy sauce
- 1/2 cup mayonnaise
- 2 tablespoons white miso
- 1 tablespoon fresh lemon juice
- 1/2 teaspoons black pepper
- 2 scallions, sliced

Preparation:

1. Mix salt, butter, hot sauce, ketchup, soy sauce, miso, mayonnaise, lemon juice, and black pepper in a bowl.
2. Season the cauliflower florets with the marinade and mix well.
3. Place the florets in the Ninja Foodi Smart XL grill.
4. Cover the Ninja Foodi Grill's hood, select the Manual Mode, set the temperature to 350 degrees F and bake the florets on the "Bake Mode" for 5-10 minutes per side.
5. Serve warm.

Serving Suggestion: Serve the cauliflower steaks with tomato sauce or guacamole.

Variation Tip: Add cheese on top of the grilled cauliflower.

Nutritional Information Per Serving:

Calories 391 | Fat 2.2g |Sodium 276mg | Carbs 27.7g | Fiber 0.9g | Sugar 1.4g | Protein 8.8g

Grilled Greens and Cheese on Toast

Prep Time: 15 minutes.

Cook Time: 36 minutes.

Serves: 4

Ingredients:

- 2 tablespoons olive oil
- 1 bunch, kale, stems removed
- 1/2 teaspoons kosher salt
- 1/2 teaspoons black pepper
- 6 oz. cherry tomatoes
- 1/2 lb. Halloumi cheese, sliced
- 1 lemon, halved crosswise
- 4 thick slices of country-style bread
- 1 large garlic clove, peeled, halved

Preparation:

1. Toss kale with olive oil, salt, black pepper, tomatoes, lemon juice, and garlic.
2. Place the tomatoes and kale in the Ninja Foodi Smart XL grill.
3. Cover the Ninja Foodi Grill's hood, select the Manual Mode, set the temperature to 350 degrees F and grill the tomatoes on the "Grill Mode" for 5 minutes per side.
4. Grill the kale leaves for 2-3 minutes per side.
5. Transfer the veggies to a bowl.
6. Grill the bread slices for 4-5 minutes per side.
7. Grill the cheese slices for 3-5 minutes per side.
8. Divide the veggies and cheese on top of the bread slices.
9. Serve warm.

Serving Suggestion: Serve the bread slices with roasted mushrooms.

Variation Tip: Add lemon zest and lemon juice on top for better taste.

Nutritional Information Per Serving:

Calories 324 | Fat 5g | Sodium 432mg | Carbs 13.1g | Fiber 0.3g | Sugar 1g | Protein 5.7g

Jalapeño Poppers with Smoked Gouda

Prep Time: 15 minutes.

Cook Time: 10 minutes.

Serves: 6

Ingredients:

- 12 large jalapeño chiles
- 4 ounces cream cheese
- 1 cup smoked Gouda, shredded
- Salt, to taste
- Chopped fresh cilantro for serving

Preparation:

1. Cut the jalapenos chiles in half and remove the seeds.
2. Mix cream cheese, gouda, and salt in a bowl.
3. Stuff this cheese mixture in the chilies.
4. Place the chiles in the Ninja Foodi Smart XL grill.
5. Cover the Ninja Foodi Grill's hood, select the Manual Mode, set the temperature to 350 degrees F and grill them on the "Grill Mode" for 5 minutes.
6. Garnish with cilantro and serve warm.

Serving Suggestion: Serve the peppers with crispy bacon.

Variation Tip: Add shredded chicken to the filling.

Nutritional Information Per Serving:

Calories 136 | Fat 10g |Sodium 249mg | Carbs 8g | Fiber 2g | Sugar 3g | Protein 4g

Grilled Watermelon, Feta, and Tomato Salad

Prep Time: 15 minutes.

Cook Time: 10 minutes.

Serves: 8

Ingredients:

- 1 tablespoon olive oil
- 1 (4-pounds) watermelon, cut into slices
- 1 teaspoon salt
- 4 heirloom tomatoes, sliced
- 1/2 teaspoon black pepper
- 6 ounces feta, sliced

Preparation:

1. Season the tomatoes and watermelon with olive oil, salt, and black pepper.

2. Place the watermelons in the Ninja Foodi Smart XL grill.

3. Cover the Ninja Foodi Grill's hood, select the Manual Mode, set the temperature to 400 degrees F and grill them on the "Grill Mode" for 2 minutes per side.

4. Transfer the watermelons to a plate and grill the tomatoes for 3 minutes per side.

5. Transfer the tomatoes to the watermelon plate.

6. Add feta cheese on top.

7. Serve.

Serving Suggestion: Serve the salad with fresh herbs on top.

Variation Tip: Add canned corn to the salad.

Nutritional Information Per Serving:

Calories 351 | Fat 19g |Sodium 412mg | Carbs 43g | Fiber 0.3g | Sugar 1g | Protein 23g

Dessert Recipes

Grilled Chocolate Sandwiches

Prep Time: 15 minutes.

Cook Time: 8 minutes.

Serves: 6

Ingredients:

- 12 (1/2-inch-thick) challah bread slices
- 3 tablespoons cherry preserves
- 2 (4-ounce) chocolate bars, each cut into thirds
- 1/3 cup unsalted butter, melted
- Confectioners' sugar, for garnish

Preparation:

1. Brush six bread slices with cherry preserves and divide the chocolate on top.
2. Place the remaining bread slices on top and brush the sandwiches with butter.
3. Place the sandwiches in the Ninja Foodi Smart XL grill.
4. Cover the Ninja Foodi Grill's hood, select the Manual Mode, set the temperature to 375 degrees F and grill them on the "Grill Mode" for 4 minutes per side.
5. Garnish with sugar and serve.

Serving Suggestion: Serve the sandwiches with chocolate dip.

Variation Tip: Add any fruit preserve for change of taste.

Nutritional Information Per Serving:

Calories 361 | Fat 10g |Sodium 218mg | Carbs 56g | Fiber 10g | Sugar 30g | Protein 14g

Grilled Pears with Cinnamon Drizzle

Prep Time: 15 minutes.

Cook Time: 14 minutes.

Serves: 3

Ingredients:

- 3 ripe pears
- 2 tablespoons honey
- 1 tablespoon cinnamon
- 1/4 cup pecans, chopped
- coconut oil
- sea salt

Preparation:

1. Peel and cut the pears into quarters.
2. Toss pears with honey, cinnamon, and coconut oil.
3. Place the pears in the Ninja Foodi Smart XL grill.
4. Cover the Ninja Foodi Grill's hood, select the Manual Mode, set the temperature to 375 degrees F and grill them on the "Grill Mode" for 7 minutes per side.
5. Garnish with pecans and sea salt.
6. Serve.

Serving Suggestion: Serve the pears with fresh berries on top.

Variation Tip: Add crushed nuts to give the pears a crunchy texture.

Nutritional Information Per Serving:

Calories 118 | Fat 20g |Sodium 192mg | Carbs 23.7g | Fiber 0.9g | Sugar 19g | Protein 5.2g

-

Marshmallow Stuffed Banana

Prep Time: 15 minutes.

Cook Time: 10 minutes.

Serves: 2

Ingredients:

- ¼ cup of chocolate chips
- 1 banana
- ¼ cup mini marshmallows

Preparation:

1. Place a peeled banana over a 12 x 12-inch foil sheet.
2. Make a slit in the banana lengthwise and stuff this slit with chocolate chips and marshmallows.
3. Wrap the foil around the banana and seal it.
4. Place the banana in the Ninja Foodi Smart XL grill.
5. Cover the Ninja Foodi Grill's hood, select the Manual Mode, set the temperature to 375 degrees F and cook on the "Bake Mode" for 5 minutes.
6. Unwrap and serve.

Serving Suggestion: Serve the marshmallows with a scoop of vanilla cream on top.

Variation Tip: Add chopped nuts to the marshmallows.

Nutritional Information Per Serving:

Calories 248 | Fat 16g |Sodium 95mg | Carbs 38.4g | Fiber 0.3g | Sugar 10g | Protein 14.1g

Apricots with Brioche

Prep Time: 15 minutes.

Cook Time: 2 minutes.

Serves: 8

Ingredients:

- 8 ripe apricots
- 2 tablespoon butter
- 2 tablespoon sugar
- 4 slice brioches, diced
- 2 tablespoon Honey
- 2 cup vanilla ice cream

Preparation:

1. Toss the apricot halves with butter and sugar.
2. Place brioche slices in the Ninja Foodi Smart XL grill.
3. Cover the Ninja Foodi Grill's hood, select the Manual Mode, set the temperature to 350 degrees F and grill on the "Grill Mode" for 1 minute per side.
4. Now grill the apricots in the same grill for 1 minute per side.
5. Top these slices with apricot slices, honey, and a scoop of vanilla ice cream.
6. Serve.

Serving Suggestion: Serve the apricot brioche with chocolate or apple sauce.

Variation Tip: Dip the brioche in maple syrup.

Nutritional Information Per Serving:

Calories 117 | Fat 12g |Sodium 79mg | Carbs 24.8g | Fiber 1.1g | Sugar 18g | Protein 5g

Rum-Soaked Pineapple

Prep Time: 15 minutes.

Cook Time: 8 minutes.

Serves: 4

Ingredients:

- 1/2 cup rum
- 1/2 cup packed brown sugar
- 1 teaspoon ground cinnamon
- 1 pineapple, cored and sliced
- cooking spray
- Vanilla ice cream

Preparation:

1. Mix run with cinnamon and brown sugar in a suitable bowl.

2. Pour this mixture over the pineapple rings and mix well.

3. Let them soak for 15 minutes, and flip the pineapples after 7 minutes.

4. Place the pineapple slices in the Ninja Foodi Smart XL grill.

5. Cover the Ninja Foodi Grill's hood, select the Manual Mode, set the temperature to 375 degrees F and grill on the "Grill Mode" for 4 minutes per side.

6. Serve with ice cream scoop on top.

Serving Suggestion: Serve the pineapple with creamy frosting on top.

Variation Tip: Add chopped pecans to the grilled pineapples.

Nutritional Information Per Serving:

Calories 195 | Fat 3g |Sodium 355mg | Carbs 20g | Fiber 1g | Sugar 25g | Protein 1g

Cinnamon grilled Peaches

Prep Time: 15 minutes.

Cook Time: 2 minutes.

Serves: 4

Ingredients:

- 1/4 cup salted butter
- 1 tablespoon 1 teaspoon granulated sugar
- 1/4 teaspoon cinnamon
- 4 ripe peaches, halved and pitted
- vegetable oil

Preparation:

1. Mix sugar with butter and cinnamon in a bowl until smooth.
2. Place the peaches in the Ninja Foodi Smart XL grill.
3. Cover the Ninja Foodi Grill's hood, select the Manual Mode, set the temperature to 400 degrees F and grill on the "Grill Mode" for 1 minute per side.
4. Serve the peaches with cinnamon butter on top.
5. Enjoy.

Serving Suggestion: Serve the peaches with chocolate syrup on top.

Variation Tip: Add dried raisins to garnish the grilled peaches.

Nutritional Information Per Serving:

Calories 203 | Fat 8.9g |Sodium 340mg | Carbs 24.7g | Fiber 1.2g | Sugar 11.3g | Protein 5.3g

Marshmallow Roll-Up

Prep Time: 15 minutes.

Cook Time: 10 minutes.

Serves: 2

Ingredients:

- 1 flour tortilla
- 1 handful mini marshmallows
- 1 handful of chocolate chips
- 2 graham crackers

Preparation:

1. Spread a 12x12 inch foil on a working surface.
2. Place the tortilla over this sheet and top it with graham crackers, chocolate chips, and marshmallows.
3. Roll the tortilla tightly by rolling the foil sheet.
4. Place the tortilla rolls in the Ninja Foodi Smart XL grill.
5. Cover the Ninja Foodi Grill's hood, select the Manual Mode, set the temperature to 350 degrees F and cook on the "Bake Mode" for 5 minutes per side.
6. Unwrap and slice in half.
7. Serve.

Serving Suggestion: Serve the rolls with chocolate syrup on top.

Variation Tip: Drizzle chocolate syrup on top of the rolls.

Nutritional Information Per Serving:

Calories 153 | Fat 1g |Sodium 8mg | Carbs 66g | Fiber 0.8g | Sugar 56g | Protein 1g

Berry Cobbler

Prep Time: 15 minutes.

Cook Time: 20 minutes.

Serves: 8

Ingredients:

- 2 cans (21 oz.) blueberry pie filling
- 1-1/4 cups water
- 1/2 cup canola oil
- 1 (8 oz.) package cake mix
- Vanilla ice cream

Preparation:

1. First, mix the cake mix with oil and water in a bowl until smooth.
2. Place the foil packet on a working surface and add pie filling.
3. Spread the cake mix on top of the filling.
4. Cover the foil packet and seal it.
5. Place the packet in the Ninja Foodi Smart XL grill.
6. Cover the Ninja Foodi Grill's hood, select the Manual Mode, set the temperature to 350 degrees F and cook on Bake Mode for 20 minutes.
7. Serve fresh with vanilla ice cream on top.

Serving Suggestion: Serve the cobbler with blueberry syrup on top.

Variation Tip: Add crushed walnuts or pecans to the filling.

Nutritional Information Per Serving:

Calories 198 | Fat 14g |Sodium 272mg | Carbs 34g | Fiber 1g | Sugar 9.3g | Protein 1.3g

Fruit Kabobs

Prep Time: 15 minutes.

Cook Time: 7 minutes.

Serves: 4

Ingredients:

- 1 tablespoon butter
- 1/2 cup apricot preserves
- 1 tablespoon water
- 1/8 teaspoon ground cinnamon
- 1/8 teaspoon ground nutmeg
- 3 nectarines, quartered
- 3 peaches, quartered
- 3 plums, quartered
- 1 loaf (10-3/4 oz.) pound cake, cubed

Preparation:

1. Take the first five ingredients in a small saucepan and stir cook for 3 minutes on medium heat.
2. Alternately thread the pound cake and fruits on the skewers.
3. Brush these skewers with the apricot mixture.
4. Place the skewers in the Ninja Foodi Smart XL grill.
5. Cover the Ninja Foodi Grill's hood, select the Manual Mode, set the temperature to 370 degrees F and grill on the "Grill Mode" for 2 minutes per side.
6. Cook the skewers in batches.
7. Serve.

Serving Suggestion: Serve the fruits with cream cheese dip

Variation Tip: Soak the cake cubes in orange juice before grilling.

Nutritional Information Per Serving:

Calories 159 | Fat 3g |Sodium 277mg | Carbs 21g | Fiber 1g | Sugar 9g | Protein 2g

Banana Skewers

Prep Time: 15 minutes.

Cook Time: 6 minutes.

Serves: 2

Ingredients:

- 1 loaf (10 3/4 oz.) cake, cubed
- 2 large bananas, one-inch slices
- 1/4 cup butter, melted
- 2 tablespoons brown sugar
- 1/2 teaspoon vanilla extract
- 1/8 teaspoon ground cinnamon
- 4 cups butter pecan ice cream
- 1/2 cup butterscotch ice cream topping
- 1/2 cup chopped pecans, toasted

Preparation:

1. Thread the cake and bananas over the skewers alternately.
2. Whisk butter with cinnamon, vanilla, and brown sugar in a small bowl.
3. Brush this mixture over the skewers liberally.
4. Place the banana skewers in the Ninja Foodi Smart XL grill.
5. Cover the Ninja Foodi Grill's hood, select the Manual Mode, set the temperature to 310 degrees F and grill on the "Grill Mode" for 3 minutes per side.
6. Serve with ice cream, pecan, and butterscotch topping on top.

Serving Suggestion: Serve the skewers with maple syrup on top.

Variation Tip: Add crushed chocolate on top of the skewers.

Nutritional Information Per Serving:
Calories 245 | Fat 14g |Sodium 122mg | Carbs 23.3g | Fiber 1.2g | Sugar 12g | Protein 4.3g

30-Days Meal Plan:

Week 1

Day 1:

Breakfast: Grilled Bruschetta

Lunch: Piri Piri Chicken

Snack: Cob with Pepper Butter

Dinner: Chili-Spiced Ribs

Dessert: Grilled Chocolate Sandwiches

Day 2:

Breakfast: Grilled Chicken Tacos

Lunch: Grilled Chicken with Grapes

Snack: Grilled Eggplant

Dinner: Shrimp with Tomatoes

Dessert: Grilled Pears with Cinnamon Drizzle

Day 3:

Breakfast: Grilled French Toast

Lunch: Grilled Chicken Thighs with Pickled Peaches

Snack: Tarragon Asparagus

Dinner: Grilled Shrimp with Miso Butter

Dessert: Marshmallow Stuffed Banana

Day 4:

Breakfast: Sausage with Eggs

Lunch: Grilled Red Curry Chicken

Snack: Grilled Butternut Squash

Dinner: Clams with Horseradish-Tabasco Sauce

Dessert: Apricots with Brioche

Day 5:

Breakfast: Coffee Glazed Bagels

Lunch: Chicken Kebabs with Currants

Snack: Honey Glazed Bratwurst

Dinner: Citrus-Soy Squid

Dessert: Rum-Soaked Pineapple

Day 6:

Breakfast: Portobello Mushrooms Bruschetta

Lunch: Grilled Chicken Breasts with Grapefruit Glaze

Snack: Chicken Salad with Blueberry Vinaigrette

Dinner: Pistachio Pesto Shrimp

Dessert: Cinnamon grilled Peaches

Day 7:

Breakfast: Avocado Eggs

Lunch: Barbecued Turkey

Snack: Grilled Oysters with Chorizo Butter

Dinner: Shrimp Stuffed Sole

Dessert: Marshmallow Roll-Up

Week 2

Day 1:

Breakfast: Bacon-Herb Grit

Lunch: Chicken with Grilled Apples

Snack: Cob with Pepper Butter

Dinner: Beef Chimichurri Skewers

Dessert: Fruit Kabobs

Day 2:

Breakfast: Grilled Bruschetta

Lunch: Tomato Turkey Burgers

Snack: Grilled Eggplant

Dinner: Salmon Lime Burgers

Dessert: Grilled Chocolate Sandwiches

Day 3:

Breakfast: Grilled Chicken Tacos

Lunch: Bourbon Drumsticks

Snack: Tarragon Asparagus

Dinner: Lemon-Garlic Salmon

Dessert: Grilled Pears with Cinnamon Drizzle

Day 4:

Breakfast: Grilled French Toast

Lunch: Sriracha Wings

Snack: Grilled Butternut Squash

Dinner: Blackened Salmon

Dessert: Marshmallow Stuffed Banana

Day 5:

Breakfast: Coffee Glazed Bagels

Lunch: Montreal Chicken Sandwiches

Snack: Honey Glazed Bratwurst

Dinner: Salmon Packets

Dessert: Apricots with Brioche

Day 6:

Breakfast: Portobello Mushrooms Bruschetta

Lunch: Spinach Turkey Burgers

Snack: Chicken Salad with Blueberry Vinaigrette

Dinner: Lamb Skewers

Dessert: Rum-Soaked Pineapple

Day 7:

Breakfast: Avocado Eggs

Lunch: Chicken and Tomatoes

Snack: Grilled Oysters with Chorizo Butter

Dinner: Crusted Beef Burger

Dessert: Cinnamon grilled Peaches

Week 3

Day 1:

Breakfast: Coffee Glazed Bagels

Lunch: Grilled Watermelon, Feta, and Tomato Salad

Snack: Cob with Pepper Butter

Dinner: Beef with Pesto

Dessert: Marshmallow Roll-Up

Day 2:

Breakfast: Portobello Mushrooms Bruschetta

Lunch: Southwestern Potato Salad

Snack: Grilled Eggplant

Dinner: Korean Beef Steak

Dessert: Grilled Chocolate Sandwiches

Day 3:

Breakfast: Coffee Glazed Bagels

Lunch: Cajun Green Beans

Snack: Tarragon Asparagus

Dinner: Fajita Skewers

Dessert: Grilled Pears with Cinnamon Drizzle

Day 4:

Breakfast: Grilled Bruschetta

Lunch: Grilled Cauliflower with Miso Mayo

Snack: Grilled Butternut Squash

Dinner: Raspberry Pork Chops

Dessert: Marshmallow Stuffed Banana

Day 5:

Breakfast: Grilled Chicken Tacos

Lunch: Grilled Greens and Cheese on Toast

Snack: Honey Glazed Bratwurst

Dinner: Ham Pineapple Skewers

Dessert: Apricots with Brioche

Day 6:

Breakfast: Grilled French Toast

Lunch: Grilled Potato Rounds

Snack: Chicken Salad with Blueberry Vinaigrette

Dinner: Sweet Chipotle Ribs

Dessert: Rum-Soaked Pineapple

Day 7:

Breakfast: Sausage with Eggs

Lunch: Vegetable Orzo Salad

Snack: Grilled Oysters with Chorizo Butter

Dinner: Pork with Salsa

Dessert: Cinnamon grilled Peaches

Week 4

Day 1:

Breakfast: Grilled Bruschetta

Lunch: Piri Piri Chicken

Snack: Cob with Pepper Butter

Dinner: Chili-Spiced Ribs

Dessert: Grilled Chocolate Sandwiches

Day 2:

Breakfast: Grilled Chicken Tacos

Lunch: Grilled Chicken with Grapes

Snack: Grilled Eggplant

Dinner: Shrimp with Tomatoes

Dessert: Grilled Pears with Cinnamon Drizzle

Day 3:

Breakfast: Grilled French Toast

Lunch: Grilled Chicken Thighs with Pickled Peaches

Snack: Tarragon Asparagus

Dinner: Grilled Shrimp with Miso Butter

Dessert: Marshmallow Stuffed Banana

Day 4:

Breakfast: Grilled French Toast

Lunch: Sriracha Wings

Snack: Grilled Butternut Squash

Dinner: Blackened Salmon

Dessert: Marshmallow Stuffed Banana

Day 5:

Breakfast: Coffee Glazed Bagels

Lunch: Montreal Chicken Sandwiches

Snack: Honey Glazed Bratwurst

Dinner: Salmon Packets

Dessert: Apricots with Brioche

Day 6:

Breakfast: Portobello Mushrooms Bruschetta

Lunch: Spinach Turkey Burgers

Snack: Chicken Salad with Blueberry Vinaigrette

Dinner: Lamb Skewers

Dessert: Rum-Soaked Pineapple

Day 7:

Breakfast: Avocado Eggs

Lunch: Chicken and Tomatoes

Snack: Grilled Oysters with Chorizo Butter

Dinner: Crusted Beef Burger

Dessert: Cinnamon grilled Peaches

Conclusion

The Ninja Foodi Smart XL Grill gives you an amazing experience of convenient indoor grilling. Just as the Ninja foodi guarantees effective grilling with minimal supervision, this cookbook ensures that you get the most out of this Ninja Foodi smart grill by understanding its smart features and by learning and trying all the indoor grilling recipes, including morning meals, meaty treats, poultry dishes, seafood, snacks, and desserts, which are all shared in each section of this cookbook. With a single read of this cookbook, all the Ninja Foodi smart grill beginners will be able to learn to use this multipurpose grill up to its full potential.

Ninja Foodi Smart Grill is nothing but convenience for those who love to enjoy nicely grilled food but too busy to set up an outdoor grill. It has brought innovation right at our fingertips by bringing all the necessary cooking in a one-touch digital device. It is simple to manage and control. And what makes the Ninja foodi grill apart from other electric grills is the diversity of options it provides for cooking all in a single pot. The ceramic coated interior and accessories make grilling an effortless experience. This cookbook puts the idea of the electric grill into perspective by discussing the basics of using the Ninja Foodi Smart Grill. The company has launched the appliance with only one aim that is to provide convenient grilling for all. Try the flavorsome grilling recipes in your Ninja Food grills and experience good taste with an amazing aroma, all with little effort and lesser time.

It's about time that you pick the best of these indoor grilling recipes and spread the aromas all around you. The Ninja food grill will surely make your grilling experience enjoyable and fun. This grill meets all your grilling, baking, dehydrating, and air frying needs. Remember that the Ninja grill quickly preheats, so keep your food ready before you switch on the appliance. Add the food to the grill and then let it do its magic. You will have juicy meaty treats and veggies grilled in no time, without any irritating smoke or charcoal mess.

CPSIA information can be obtained
at www.ICGtesting.com
Printed in the USA
BVHW051941301221
625197BV00005B/329